Stor.

Oxford
Castle

-⊱⊰-

From Dungeon to Dunghill

MARK DAVIES

Oxford Towpath Press
2005

© Mark Davies 2005

ISBN O 9535593 3 5

A catalogue record for this book is available from the British Library.

Published by Oxford Towpath Press
c/o Mark Davies,
12 Hythe Bridge Arm, Oxford Canal,
Oxford OX1 2TA
TEL: 01865 798254

Towpathpress@btopenworld.com

Designed by Bryony Newhouse

Printed by Information Press, Eynsham

Image on front cover: A drawing by Daniel Harris
for Edward King's *Vestiges of Oxford Castle* (1796).

Contents

➤➤◄◄

Preface

In December 2005, the public will be allowed free access to the precincts of the former Oxford Castle for the first time in its history, as the site is converted to a hotel, restaurants, a heritage centre, and public open space. This book marks that moment with a look at the experiences of some of the men and women who had occasion to know the place under rather different circumstances – namely as either prisoners or as their guardians. Most of those described lived from the middle of the seventeenth century, when the earliest eye-witness accounts of the prison emerge, to the beginning of the nineteenth, when the tenure of Daniel Harris, the most influential of all the Oxford gaolers, came to an end. His was a period marked by fundamental and long-lasting changes to both the prison's physical appearance and in general attitudes to the sentencing and treatment of prisoners. It seems an apt point at which to stop, in advance of the complexities of the Victorian era to come.

The three principal sources used in compiling this history were a) the records of the Oxfordshire Quarter Sessions courts stored at the Oxfordshire Record Office, b) Oxford's weekly newspaper, *Jackson's Oxford Journal* (first published in May 1753), and c) contemporary broadsheets, pamphlets, and other publications held mainly at the Bodleian Library, Oxford.

Of the three, the quarter sessions records are the most informative. These county magistrates' courts were held four times a year, with the Epiphany sessions in January, followed by those of Easter, Trinity, and Michaelmas at intervals of 12 weeks or so. The minute books for all the sessions from Easter 1683 to Michaelmas 1830 survive, as too do most of the original documents considered at each session. The most revealing of these are the bills submitted by various gaolers and tradesmen, appeals for clemency from impoverished prisoners, and the lists (known as Calendars) of prisoners held in the castle at the time of each session. From these documents it is possible to deduce much about the condition of the castle buildings and about the regimes which were responsible for their upkeep. But of rather greater interest is the light these documents shed on the prisoners' treatment and their backgrounds, on their attitude to authority and to each other, and on both the logic and logistics of transportation to the American colonies. Additionally, much new or confirmatory detail emerges in relation to the original crimes of inmates, their sentences, and length of incarceration.

Yet all this fascinating detail would have remained largely obscured had it not been for the extraordinary efforts of Canon Oldfield in transcribing, indexing, and cross-indexing the 38,600 documents which comprise the quarter sessions bundles. He completed this immense task in September 1926. As he did so without any obvious errors, my faith in his accuracy (and indeed his ability to decipher archaic handwriting much more successfully than I!) has meant that on occasions it is Oldfield's transcriptions that I have relied on, rather than the primary source.

In *A Proposal for Making Effectual Provision for the Poor* (1753), Henry Fielding wrote: "The sufferings of the poor are indeed less observed than their misdeeds." This book is a humble attempt to rectify that situation a little – though misdeeds there are aplenty too! From the evidence available, it is apparent that many of the prisoners described were luckless or desperate victims of circumstance, rather than malevolent or incorrigible miscreants. As a consequence, many who found themselves on the very public platform of the gallows were lauded by the masses as champions of the down-trodden, or as rebels against an overbearing system of law and morality. It became tempting to think of everyone who is featured in this book in these terms (especially in those cases where the establishment press appeared to be of the same opinion), attributing to them a moral fibre and resilience of spirit which could be far from the truth. I have, I hope, resisted that trap, however, on the basis that "the truth will not appear altogether void of charms, nor … less pleasing for being within reach of probability", as the celebrated Oxford prisoner Peter le Maitre said of his memoirs. In other words, the bare facts already contain sufficient drama to make fanciful elaboration unnecessary.

Throughout the book, named streets or parishes can be assumed to be in Oxford, unless otherwise stated, and similarly all villages to be in Oxfordshire (bearing in mind that the River Thames constituted the county border in times past, meaning that those parts of modern Oxfordshire which lie to the south or west of the river were formerly part of Berkshire, as FIGURE 1 shows). In quoted text from both printed and handwritten sources, the initial capital letters used on all nouns have been edited down. On account of the thorough indexing of both the Oxfordshire Quarter Sessions documents and of *Jackson's Oxford Journal*, and the comprehensive Bodleian database, it was not thought necessary to provide exact references for all quotations.

ACKNOWLEDGEMENTS

My main thanks go to Catherine Robinson for her immaculate editing of an early draft, her advice and encouragement, and not least for her suggestion for the book's sub-title. Thanks are also due to Bryony Newhouse, for her further refinement of the title (as well as for her self-evident skilful design work and patience). My research was made all the more pleasant and meaningful by the ever-helpful staff of the Oxfordshire Record Office (in Cowley, Oxford), the Centre for Oxfordshire Studies (in the Westgate Library, Oxford), and the Modern Papers Room at the Bodleian Library, Oxford. Others to whom I am grateful are Carl Boardman and Tom Hassall, Julian Munby and Dan Poore of Oxford Archaeology, and Sanders of Oxford.

Mark Johnstone Davies
"Bill the Lizard", Oxford,
November 2005

THE AUTHOR

Mark Davies has lived on a narrowboat in central Oxford since 1992. He has published three previous books under the imprint of Oxford Towpath Press. These are *Our Canal In Oxford* (1999) and *A Towpath Walk In Oxford* (2001), both co-written with Catherine Robinson, and *The Abingdon Waterturnpike Murder* (2003).

To complement the books, Mark runs walks and talks for a variety of local interest groups, public institutions, and academic bodies, based on the themes of: the social history of the Oxford Canal and River Thames in Oxford, on the literary relevance of Oxford's waterways, and on eighteenth-century crime and punishment.

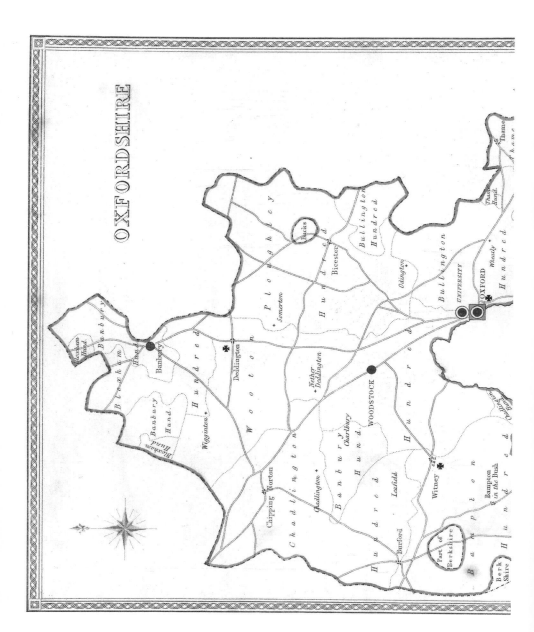

OXFORDSHIRE

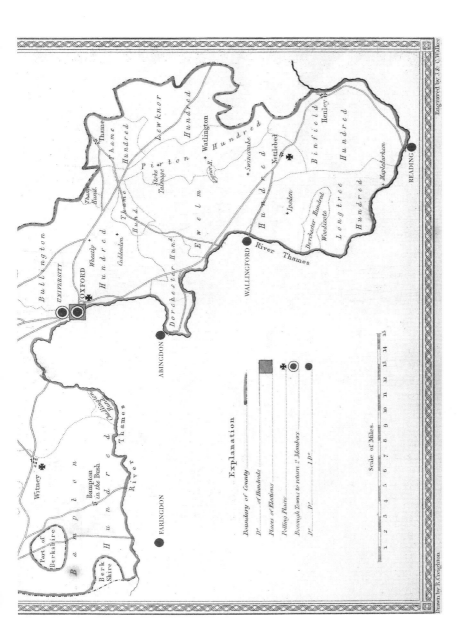

FIGURE 1: Map of Oxfordshire engraved for R.K. Dawson's 1832 *Boundaries Commission*. The locations of Abingdon, Faringdon, and Wallingford (all now in Oxfordshire), and Reading have been added for clarity.

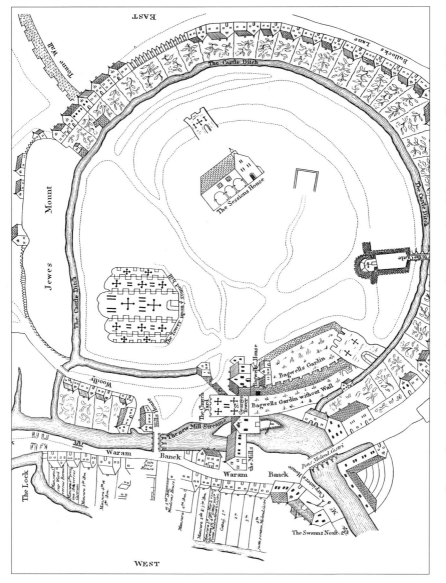

FIGURE 2: Extract from a copy of an early seventeenth-century plan of the castle and mill stream held at Christ Church. Of note is "The Tower upon ye round hill", "The Sessions House" (scene of the Black Assize), and the gallows to the south of it. Bagwell's house refers to Thomas Bagwell, keeper of the gaol in 1617.

CHAPTER ONE

KEEPERS AND CUSTODIANS

By the standards of many English castles, Oxford's has enjoyed a relatively uneventful past. Only rarely has it featured in matters of national importance, but its role as a county prison is a fascinating one, throwing light on the lives of the ordinary – and sometimes extraordinary – citizens who found themselves, however briefly, enclosed within its walls. Most of those who are featured in the following chapters lived in the eighteenth century, but a brief survey of the castle's early history will help to set their exploits in context.

The earliest mention of Oxford occurs in The Anglo-Saxon Chronicle of 912, when the settlement was important enough to be ranked with London as key to King Edward the Elder's defence of Wessex against the Danes. The Thames was already a well-used waterway, enabling communication between London and important towns such as Wallingford, Abingdon, and Oxford, so control of the river was of essential strategic importance. Oxford's original Saxon fort was therefore positioned to give vantage over what was then the main course of the Thames, called today Castle Mill Stream (see FIGURE 2).

The Norman castle

→>‹‹

The Norman conquerors who arrived in 1066 strengthened the Saxon site, William I having appointed Robert D'Oyley (or D'Oilly) as the first custodian of Oxford Castle. D'Oyley constructed a keep on top of the mound, with a surrounding moat and stone walls incorporating six defensive towers (see FIGURE 3). The work was completed in 1071. Only the tower of St George remains, preserved on account of its special importance as protection for the adjacent mill from which the name Castle Mill Stream derives.

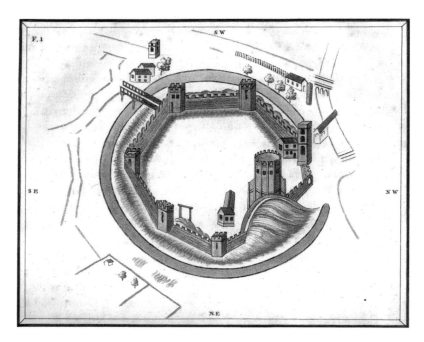

FIGURE 3: Drawing based on Ralph Agas' map of 1578 by the gaoler Daniel Harris for Edward King's *Vestiges of Oxford Castle* (1796). The orientation is unusual, with north east at the bottom and south east at the top, so that the Castle Mill Stream appears to the right. The main entrance to the castle is to the south, through a bridge over the moat.

The keep, originally of wood, later of stone, constituted a powerful symbol of Norman dominance, visible to the whole neighbourhood. The local population submitted unwillingly to D'Oyley's stringent methods, and it seems likely that the castle would have doubled as a prison for the most persistently unwilling almost immediately. However, it was not until early in the reign of Henry III, who succeeded in 1216, that a portion of the castle was officially designated as a prison, expressly for the incarceration of rebellious clerks (students) from the University. In 1239 it became the common gaol for the county, and housed the shire and assizes courts until the eventful Black Assize of 1577 (see Chapter Four), having had only minimal military importance from the early fourteenth century. From records held at the National Archives at Kew, the names of two early Oxford gaolers emerge: John Crokston, from 1486 to 1529, and John Wells, from 1538 to 1544. The castle site was sold to speculators in 1611 by James I. A plan from about this time (see FIGURE 2) shows domestic houses had infiltrated the edges of the site. The prison consisted of a small cluster of buildings next to St George's Tower, including that of the keeper of the gaol, Thomas Bagwell (1576?–?), who presumably succeeded John Bagwell (who was buried at St Thomas' Church on 13 July 1605) and was still the incumbent in 1625. In 1613 the site was purchased by Christ Church, the richest of the Oxford colleges, which leased it to a succession of Oxford tradesmen on behalf of the county justices for the best part of the next two centuries.

"Inhumane, unspeakable, and unheard-of usage": The Civil War

→>-<+-

The castle assumed brief military importance during the Civil War, when Oxford was at the centre of the Royalist cause for nearly four years, from the day when Charles I entered Oxford in October 1642 to his surrender to Oliver Cromwell's Parliamentarians in June 1646. The first eye-witness accounts of conditions for prisoners appear at about this time – a time when the most inoffensive of men could find themselves behind bars, with the most inappropriate of men in charge of them!

A clergyman called Edward Wirely was held in the castle at the end of 1641, along with numerous other men suspected of opposing the monarchy. In *The Prisoners' Report*, printed on the authority of the House of Commons on 20 March 1642, he identified two men named Smith, both "Marshalls of his Majestie's army", as responsible for the unnecessarily harsh treatment imposed on him and his companions. William Smith, "a flaxen-haired man", was Provost Marshall General, and Thomas Smith was "Marshall of the horse, a tall big fellow, and has been formerly (as some say) a fencer, a man of a bloody minde also".[*] Held by the former in cramped, insanitary conditions, Wirely wrote that the only relief was that some gentlemen "had their libertie sometimes to walk in the castle court (a little stinking yard and the onely place that the prisoners had to ease nature), Smith not permitting any, no not with a keeper, to go to any other upon that necessitie".

Commoners were treated still worse. 180 Republican survivors of a battle at Marlborough were brought to Oxford and "put up in to an high tower, and lodged upon the boards: the rooms were so stuffed with them that they could not lie downe by one another". As a minister of religion, Wirely was allowed special access to these men, but by the same measure exposed himself to accusations of spreading dissent. William Smith had Wirely beaten for encouraging the prisoners to rebel, and paraded him through the town on market day, en route to incarceration in the dungeon of the city bridewell (prison). There conditions were still more intolerable.[†] It was so crowded that he had to sit upright at night, at the bottom of the dungeon stairs. "In some places of it a man might have gon almost

---

[*] A "fencer" implies Smith fought for money at fairs or public shows. Wirely's reference suggests it was considered a less than honourable occupation.

[†] The bridewell or city gaol (called the Bocardo by at least 1391) stood at the North Gate near St Michael's Church, and was intended mainly for holding residents of the city accused of relatively minor misdemeanours. The Bocardo's most famous prisoners were bishops Thomas Cranmer, Nicholas Ridley, and Hugh Latimer, who were held there prior to their executions in 1555 and 1556.

over his shoes in pisse", because "we had no place for the easement of nature but that where wee were in, both night and day, also sick persons were forced in the same place to empty their stomacks, so that the stinch of the place was enough to poyson us". Fortunately he escaped three weeks later with about 40 others, including the former bridewell keeper himself, whom Smith had thrown into his own dungeon for showing too much compassion to the men under his charge.

The merciless regime was not improved by the arrival in Oxford of the king. In a printed letter dated 13 January 1643, "a poore gentleman prisoner" described "a true relation of the most woeful and miserable state and condition of these distressed prisoners taken by his Majesties forces, and detained and kept in the castle at Oxford". On this occasion it was the other Smith, Thomas, who was blamed, the letter complaining specifically of "the inhumane, unspeakable, and unheard-of usage of their keeper or gaoler Captaine Thomas Smith, the Marshall General". As examples of this "usage" the writer stated:

> We endure cold, hunger, and nakedness, fetters, bolts, and irons, our beds we lie on, are stuft with feathers longer than our arms and coverlets wanting, and the hard boards our bedsteads. We are so thrust and packed up together, and in such close and small rooms, that wanting roome for us to lie, some of us are inforced perforce to stand in woeful manner until the residue take their unquiet rest.

He concluded with the kind of damning yet erudite assessment of Thomas Smith which surely only an Oxford prisoner could compose. It is hard to imagine any other city where a gaoler might be branded "a man composed of naught but wickedness, begot by an Incubus, nursed by a Succubus, or else the very spawne of Cerebus, more fitter for the gaoler of Devils than a keeper of Christians"!

With the execution of Charles I in 1649, Oxford's military importance was well and truly over. The additional fortifications erected during the Civil War were removed in 1652 – "in four dayes' space" according to the Oxford diarist and historian, Anthony Wood, and "in a whimsey quite pulled down and demolished". The castle became exclusively the common gaol and house of correction for the county from then on. It was still under the control of Christ Church, and the system of leasing the buildings to individuals who received no salary, but ran the prison as a business, was resumed. It was this arrangement which pertained in 1687, when the earliest surviving records of the Oxfordshire Quarter Sessions (held at the Oxfordshire County Record Office) begin to reveal the story of the castle and its temporary residents in any consistent detail.

The earliest gaolers are named as Mrs Elizabeth Thorpe (in 1688) and Mr Robert Thorpe (in 1691 – although J. M. Davenport, in *Notes as to Oxford Castle*, puts his appointment at about 1670). Mrs Thorpe at least seems to have maintained the standards of the Smiths in the 1640s, being referred to in a 1690 document as "the Devil".

The Eighteenth Century

→>-<←

THE ETTY FAMILY

In 1700 comes the first appearance of the name Etty, the family to whom Christ Church leased the castle franchise for most of the following century. The succession is unclear, but Andrew Etty, who was a minister of the church, at least by the time of his death, appears to have been the first incumbent. He was followed by Marmaduke Etty (who is referred to in the quarter sessions documentation from 1721 to 1730), Mrs Elizabeth Etty (from 1732 to 1740), and then Charles Etty (from 1739 to 1742).

The quarter sessions court regularly considered appeals from poor prisoners unable to survive on the paltry allowance provided by law, and especially from debtors, for whom no allowance at all was made. Two examples from the period of control by the Ettys are of particular interest

FIGURE 4: *Oxford Castle in Oxfordshire* pre-1772. The image is from a 1786 publication, copied from a version published in 1772. The chapel (founded by Thomas Horde) is in the centre, with the gallows nearby to the right. John Howard's observation that "the gaoler has a spacious garden" is beyond dispute!

because they allude to the condition of the buildings, which consisted at this time merely of St George's Tower, the chapel, the keeper's house, and the prison itself (see FIGURE 4).

At the Easter sessions of 1713, the magistrates were informed that the "Rev Mr Wheatley of St Johns College has for some weeks served the chapel in the castle founded by Thomas Horde [see Chapter Four] and others, and will so continue gratis if it be repaired, the roof letting in the rain everywhere". This was followed at the next sessions with a petition from some prisoners to have the chapel repaired, a request which was duly acknowledged with acceptance of William Townsend's estimate for the job, which included "an iron cramp to go through the breadth of the chapel".*

The transition from the Etty family to the next gaoling dynasty, the Wisdoms, is encapsulated in a second letter alluding to structural deficiency, written on behalf of thirteen debtors, many of whose unavoidably long stays gave them ample opportunity to observe the minutiae of the castle's internal changes. The letter was written in January 1741, asking for glass to be installed in the window of the debtors' cell. The authors pointed to a precedent of January 1738 when the debtors "then lying in the tower or common side" had successfully requested that an open window "should be glazed and that some peggs might be fixed up … to hang cloths [their clothing] upon". When the number of debtors had increased in the previous November, however, Mr Etty, "the late keeper", had been obliged to lodge some of them in a second room. Mr Wisdom, "the current keeper", was continuing to hold debtors in this room, but, much like the first one, it too had "a window without any glass on the north east side … which is at least fifty feet high whereby your petitioners who lodge in the same room are very much exposed to the inclemency of the weather to the impairing of their healths".

---

* This is presumably William Townesend (?–1739), from the family of architects and masons whose considerable influence on the architecture of the city extended over five generations, beginning with William's father, John (1648–1728), and ending with Stephen (1755–1800).

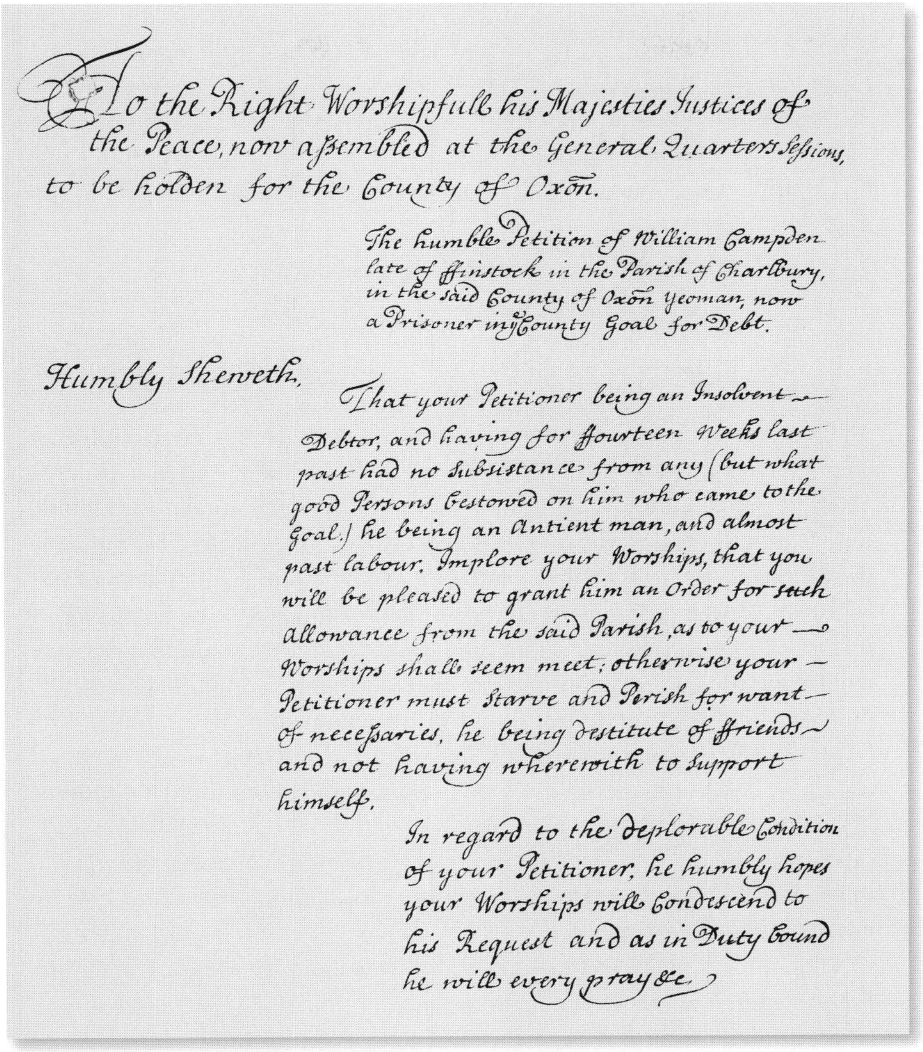

To the Right Worshipfull his Majesties Justices of the Peace, now assembled at the General Quarters Sessions, to be holden for the County of Oxon.

The humble Petition of William Campden late of ffinstock in the Parish of Charlbury, in the said County of Oxon yeoman, now a Prisoner in County Goal for Debt.

Humbly Sheweth.

That your Petitioner being an Insolvent Debtor, and having for ffourteen weeks last past had no subsistance from any (but what good Persons bestowed on him who came to the Goal) he being an Antient man, and almost past labour. Implore your Worships, that you will be pleased to grant him an Order for such allowance from the said Parish, as to your Worships shall seem meet; otherwise your Petitioner must starve and Perish for want of necessaries, he being destitute of ffriends and not having wherewith to support himself.

In regard to the deplorable Condition of your Petitioner, he humbly hopes your Worships will Condescend to his Request and as in Duty bound he will every pray &c.

FIGURE 5: An appeal to the county magistrates from "an insolvent debtor", William Campden. Considered at the quarter sessions of Michaelmas 1731, its educated style and formal politeness are typical of such requests.
[*Copyright: Oxfordshire County Record Office*]

This deferential, articulate (and successful) request contains the earliest reference to Wisdoms, the family which would occupy the keeper's role for nearly the next half century. There is no evidence of their background or suitability, but it would seem that they represented a step down in terms of status, being purely subcontracted for the role, rather than holding any legal entitlement to it, as the Etty family continued to do.

WILLIAM WISDOM (1706?–1769): GAOLER FROM 1742 TO 1769

It is difficult to assess the performances of the preceding keepers of Oxford Castle Gaol, given that the quarter sessions documentation is the only consistent source. It was during William Wisdom's long tenure as gaoler that the first issue of *Jackson's Oxford Journal* appeared, however, in May 1753, and with it an additional means of interpretation and elucidation. No doubt there were escapes and executions prior to this time, the details of which we shall never know. *Jackson's*, however, appears to have reported on all such occurrences meticulously (as will be seen in the following chapters), and the fact that the newspaper reported no escapes at all during William Wisdom's time suggests that he performed his duties diligently. He had one major factor in his favour: that he probably had relatively few prisoners to guard at any one time. His years in charge were characterised by the increasingly regular transportation of large numbers of prisoners to the plantations of north America. As the number of crimes punishable by death rose through the century, judges increasingly sought to impose this lesser penalty, so the prison population was never likely to have become excessive.

All in all, it is probably indicative of a well-run operation that the only time Wisdom's name was brought to the attention of *Jackson's* readers was when he died, in June 1769, at the age of 63. Poignantly, his widow, Ann, died exactly a week later, of "a paralitick stroke". In his 1767 will, Wisdom had left his entire estate to his wife. Because she died so soon after him, the legacy passed to Susanna (wife of John) Lambourn, the sole executrix of

Ann. Susanna Lambourn had been a witness at the only Wisdom marriage recorded in the parish registers of St Thomas' Church, when Sarah Wisdom married one John Truby on 28 May 1769, only weeks before her parents' deaths. Other Wisdom entries at St Thomas' are the baptism of William and Ann's sons Richard (1742), Aaron (1744), and Moses (1746). Of Charles (the son who succeeded William) and Solomon, future keepers of Oxford Castle Gaol, there is no record, suggesting that they were baptised elsewhere prior to 1742, and that William moved to Oxford specifically to take up the role.

CHARLES WISDOM:
GAOLER FROM 1769 TO 1774

Conditions inside the gaol seem to have deteriorated during Charles Wisdom's tenure, despite early reassurances to the contrary. Within months, it was felt necessary to advise an anxious public that rumours of an outbreak gaol distemper were false. *Jackson's* of 30 September 1769 reported that while it was true that two prisoners had died recently, "both of them were aged persons, sinking under complicated diseases". The newspaper went on to comment: "The rest of the prisoners, as well as Mr Wisdom's family, are now, and have been, in as perfect a state of health as can at any time be remembered, as are also the inhabitants of this city in general." Be that as it might, outbreaks of gaol fever and smallpox became commonplace thereafter, such that eleven deaths from smallpox occurred in 1773 alone. A contributing factor may have been the additional requirement to accommodate the city prisoners from the Bocardo, when it was demolished in 1771. This arrangement continued until a new city prison was opened at Gloucester Green in 1789. In such confined quarters, contagion was inevitable, and perhaps it was the threat of this more immediate termination of their sentences as much as the gradual deterioration of the buildings that led to the first of many subsequent escapes at this point. Notices relating to two such escapes within the space of two months (see Chapter Two) mark the transition

FIGURE 6: *St Thomas's Church* from James Ingram's 1837 *Memorials of Oxford*. As the church most closely associated with the castle, St Thomas' has seen the burials of many criminals who were executed or victims of disease, and of at least one custodian of the prison. The tree-covered Castle Mound is in the background to the right.

from Charles Wisdom to the third of his family to hold the post of keeper of the prison. In September 1774, Charles offered a reward in *Jackson's* for the recapture of Edward Clarke; in November, the name at the bottom of the announcement of William Ward's escape was Charles' presumed brother, Solomon.

SOLOMON WISDOM:
GAOLER FROM 1774 TO 1786

From available sources it is difficult to discern that much was amiss at Oxford Castle Gaol during the tenure of the first two Wisdoms. There is no hint of bad treatment (indeed, rather the opposite is suggested by the consistent high cost to the County of feeding and nursing poor prisoners), and it appears that justice was carried out in as orderly and civilised a manner as the standards of the time would allow.

Things were a lot less settled during the governorship of Solomon, the next Wisdom in line, however. This was not necessarily a reflection on Wisdom himself. There is some evidence, certainly by the time of his dismissal, that he might have abused his position, or at least been unsuited to it, but external factors conspired to make his probably the most taxing period that any keeper had known.

In 1776, transportation to America ceased as Britain's war with America intensified. As an interim measure, felons otherwise due for transportation were held on hulks in the Thames estuary, but the ships proved inadequate to accommodate the never-ending numbers of men and women so sentenced from all over the country. Oxford's was therefore not the only gaol to add extreme overcrowding to the already daunting aspects of incarceration within its walls. And the end of the war in 1783 only made matters worse, as a lack of employment for returning troops led inevitably to an increase in crime. By March 1784, for instance, there were 49 male felons in the castle, plus an indeterminate numbers of debtors, when the usual prison population was less than half that.

While Solomon Wisdom was gaoler, he received many visits from the influential prison reformer, John Howard (1726–1790). Howard had been sheriff of Bedfordshire until 1773. He had therefore been able to observe first-hand the plight of prisoners, who endured conditions of great deprivation and intimidation on account of the policy of denying gaolers any consistent means of support other than the fees paid by the prisoners themselves. Howard therefore advocated that gaolers should be paid a salary, and visited numerous prisons in the neighbouring counties between 1773 and 1775, to see if there was any precedent for this. In so doing, he discovered "scenes of calamity which I grew daily more and more anxious to alleviate". These he recorded in *The State of the Prisons in England and Wales* (published in 1777, with further editions in 1780, 1784, and 1792), in which he reproduced the words of a "celebrated" (though unnamed) author to summarise his own observations:

> The misery suffered in gaols is not half their evil; they are filled with every sort of corruption that poverty and wickedness can generate: with all the shameless and profligate enormities that can be produced by the impudence of ignominy, the rage of want, and the malignity of despair. In a prison the check of the public eye is removed; and the power of the law is spent. There are few fears, there are no blushes. The lewd inflame the more modest; the audacious harden the timid. Every one fortifies himself as he can against his own remaining sensibility, endeavouring to practice on others the arts that are practiced on himself, and to gain the applause of his associates by imitating their manners.

At Oxford, Howard noted in 1780 that the courtyard used by prisoners of both sexes measured only 29 feet by 23, the "felons' day-room or hall for *men and women* down 5 steps" was 12 feet by 15, the men's dungeon (measuring $18^{1}/_{2}$ feet by $16^{1}/_{2}$ by 1782) "down 5 more; only small apertures" and "the women's night-room $6^{1}/_{2}$ feet by 4 feet; no windows". So, there was very little space at a time when prisoners could count on long delays and therefore plenty of company. Describing the interiors, Howard said: "No infirmary: no bath: no straws: the prisoners lie in their clothes on mats. The men's dungeon swarms with vermin; yet not white-washed for many years". His final comment was a surely ironic: "The gaoler has a spacious garden."

Yet the gaoler probably needed it! It should not be forgotten that in some respects the keepers were as trapped as their charges were. As they lived in close proximity to large numbers of often desperate and violent men and women, who endured conditions of varying degrees of deprivation and squalor, it is fair to say that it was not a job for the faint-hearted! There is no evidence of any of the Oxford keepers actually being assaulted, but the fear must always have been present. When *Jackson's* noted on 28 February 1784 the foiled plan of 27 felons to seize Wisdom at locking-up time, this was doubtless not the only such occurrence. Nor probably was the incident referred to by John Howard during his visit in December 1782: "the felons day-room is paved with flat stones, in consequence of their taking up the pebbles for defence, after an attempt to escape".

But if political factors meant that Solomon Wisdom faced more severe tests in the science of gaol-keeping than either of his family predecessors, another factor was more straightforward: the deterioration of the prison's physical structure. Throughout the century, the Oxfordshire magistrates had regularly paid the bills of masons, smiths, and carpenters for repairs at the castle, at considerable cumulative cost. Eventually though, the fundamental problem had to be faced: only a complete redevelopment would solve all the difficulties. And to do so, the County concluded that complete control of the site was needed. This signalled not merely a change in the physical appearance of the buildings, but a change in attitude too. Heeding Howard's philosophy, the magistrates paid Wisdom a salary of £50 a year from the 24 June 1784, mainly, as it was stated, in lieu of the obviously lucrative right that he formerly held "of selling ale and liquor" at the gaol.* But Wisdom was steeped in the old but perfectly

---

* This was taken a step farther soon after Wisdom's dismissal. *Jackson's* of 21 April 1787 announced the magistrates' decision that "in future persons bringing beer or victuals to any of the prisoners shall be obliged to deliver the same at the turnkey's lodge, and that no person, under any pretence whatever, shall be permitted to visit the felons upon Sundays". It represented another success for John Howard, whose enthusiasm for his subject had incorporated visits to many European prisons. In 1789 he published *An Account of the Principal Lazarettos of Europe etc.* (in which he included Britain), observing that in most prisons Sunday was "a day of confusion and intoxication".

legitimate ways of accumulating wealth through the payments of the prisoners. Unable to come to terms with this new state of affairs, he would soon become a victim of them.

The sequence of change can be traced from the notices placed in *Jackson's* over these years. The earliest appears on 16 October 1784, when the paper advised that the "insufficiency and want of repairs at the castle gaol" would be considered at the next quarter sessions. Sure enough, the minutes of the magistrates' court for Epiphany 1785 contain a resolution to undertake wholesale reconstruction of the site. To do so, the County paid £331 10s to Christ Church and a further £800 in respect of the various leases (held on 40-year terms) "vested in Charles Etty Esq and others under the several wills of the Rev Andrew Etty and James Etty deceased".

The London architect William Blackburn (1750–1790) was appointed, and in *Jackson's* of 9 April 1785 the first intentions were made public with an invitation to builders and masons to tender "for making a boundary wall round the castle gaol at Oxford, and a wing to the intended bridewell to be built within the said wall". The City too was active at this time. City prisoners had of course been held at the castle ever since the demolition of the old Bocardo in 1771. Now tenders also were invited (*Jackson's* 16 July 1785) to build "a boundary wall and gaol, and a house of correction in Gloucester Green". Blackburn, whose skill was much admired by John Howard, was again the architect.

On 8 April 1786 *Jackson's* invited tenders "for building one wing of the intended gaol and house of correction and the carcase of the keeper's house" at the castle. This notice is of especial interest in that it advised that particulars could be obtained from the Clerk of Works at the castle. This is the earliest reference to such a position. Though not named, the post-holder was Daniel Harris, an extraordinary man who would soon succeed Wisdom as keeper, and have an influence on Oxford way beyond that of simply running the prison.

Daniel Harris (1761?–1840): gaoler from 1786 to 1809

-+->-<+-

The appointment of Daniel Harris marked a new breed of prison governor, as the position came to be called. The days of gaol dynasties like the Ettys and Wisdoms had passed, and with them the manipulations of a magistrature whose best interests were served by helping these families to operate at a profit, in order to reduce the cost to the county.

Harris was a more accountable public servant, paid a handsome salary more than double that of Solomon Wisdom's short-lived pay, and required to exhibit a concomitant professionalism. This he appears to have done with aplomb – although there are many hints that his mind was not always fully on the job, on account of possessing an abundance of skills which presented him with frequent, though very productive, distractions. There are no known images or descriptions of any of the Oxford gaolers of the eighteenth or earlier centuries, other than Wirely's brief details about the two Smiths. Harris is the first for whom we have any visual clues, but even they come in a less than convincing form: an unflattering caricature drawn by one of the prisoners at the instigation of Harris' soon-to-be predecessor, Solomon Wisdom (see FIGURE 7).

The drawing, showing Harris standing on top of a dunghill with the wholehearted approval of the Devil, is entitled "Daniel Damnable". The dunghill in question, as revealed by correspondence retained in the quarter sessions documents for Michaelmas 1786, was a source of dispute, the magistrates having ordered Wisdom some time earlier to move the pile of earth and rubbish from the debtors' yard. Wisdom ignored this instruction more than once, and indeed allowed the debtors to add to the dunghill "where it stopped up some drains which were made to carry off water from the foundation of the boundary wall". As a consequence, Harris, then still the Clerk of Works, was given direct orders to prevent any more earth being added. Wisdom, resentful that this youthful newcomer

FIGURE 7: *Daniel Damnable Surveying the Dunghill.* The insulting caricature drawn by
the prisoner David Gadsdon at Solomon Wisdom's "request" in 1787. The words
"cock of this dunghill" constitute an additional slight, a "dunghill cock" being
a derogatory term applied to men lacking in spirit or courage.
[*Copyright: Oxfordshire County Record Office*]

should be shown favour over himself, sought some means of revenge, and decided on ridicule as his best weapon.

Aware of the artistic talents of one of the long-term debtors, David Gadsdon, Wisdom put pressure on him to represent Harris in a ridiculous situation of some kind. Gadsdon, as his letter to the magistrates of 2 October 1786 shows, dared not refuse. His compliance came down to fear of reprisals, Gadsdon reminding the magistrates of "how ill I have been treated by Mr Wisdom" since about two years earlier, when an assault on him by Wisdom had remained unproven "by the false accusations and aspersions exhibited against me by the keeper". So, the drawing was duly produced, much to Wisdom's satisfaction, and pinned on the outside of the prison entrance, where as many people as possible might share the joke, to the irrecoverable detriment of Harris' reputation. Or so Wisdom hoped. Unfortunately for him, Gadsdon's confession had the opposite effect. Wisdom was dismissed by the magistrates, who deemed his behaviour had been "contrary to the peace and good government" of the gaol. Worse still, Harris was promoted in his place – with a hefty increase in salary to boot! But time had been running out for Wisdom in any case. His intransigence over the matter of the dunghill was not the only example of behaviour "repugnant to every plan of reform lately introduced by the magistrates", and the incident is a literally graphic demonstration of the changing times. The absolute power of the keeper over the prisoners in his charge had passed. The new breed of prison governors were required to do exactly that – govern, with a view to helping prisoners to reform, rather than simply to guard them until such time as their punishments could be effected.

So Daniel Harris, not yet 30 years old, found himself suddenly in a position of great responsibility, at a time of enormous change. There is little doubt that he was exactly the right man for the job. The practical abilities which had earned him the position of Clerk of Works made him ideal to oversee the completion of Blackburn's designs for a radically rebuilt prison. There was change afoot elsewhere in Oxford too, however, and he was soon also in demand from other authorities with construction needs in the Oxford area. These were principally the Oxford Canal Company, whose original nearby terminus (today's Worcester Street car-park) was completed by 1789 (see FIGURE 8), and the Commissioners of the Thames Navigation, who authorised considerable improvements on the river up- and downstream of Oxford from 1788 on. Harris, with convenient convict labour at his disposal, and the skills to direct that labour to best advantage, had a profound impact on both projects.*

CONVICT LABOUR IN OXFORD

Harris' enthusiasm for construction projects of all kinds was probably the salvation of many an Oxford prisoner. For although the practice of regular transportation resumed in 1787, Australia was still an unknown quantity, considerably farther away than America, and available vessels were scarce. Had Harris not contrived to involve himself in these local projects, where manual labour was in consistent demand, many prisoners would no doubt have found themselves suffering as many of their fore-runners had, in conditions of overcrowding and soul-destroying inactivity. These labour-intensive projects provided every reason to keep prisoners in Oxford, however, where many went on to learn new skills while serving their sentences, to the great satisfaction of those who preached John Howard's philosophy of rehabilitation rather than retribution. In *An Account of the Principal Lazarettos of Europe etc.*, Howard's comments reflect well on Daniel Harris:

> Here the lodges, and the gateway with the chapel over it, will be built entirely by the convicts. These were at work, and guarded only by one man, though several of them, for their *good behaviour* had their irons taken off. This proves that amongst such delinquents many are reclaimable, and not so entirely abandoned as some are apt to suppose.

* This is not the place to dwell on the pivotal role played by Harris in the fortunes of both waterways, his contribution to other capital projects for which the Oxfordshire authorities were responsible, nor his other talents as an illustrator and subsequent commercial builder and architect. Interested readers can learn more in the Oxford Towpath Press publications *A Towpath Walk In Oxford* and *The Abingdon Waterturnpike Murder.*

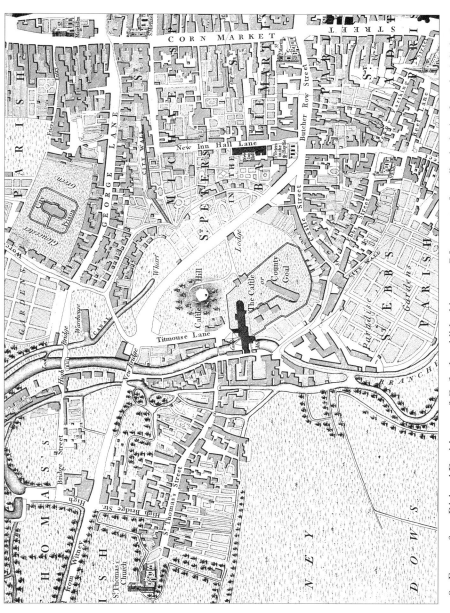

FIGURE 8: Extract from Richard Davis' map of Oxford, published in 1797. Of note are: (broadly clockwise from far left) St Thomas' Church, the Castle Mill Stream (flowing north to south), the terminus of the Oxford Canal, Gloucester Green and "Friers Entry", George Lane, Corn Market and St Michael's Church (adjacent to the former Bocardo), and New Hall Lane. Very approximately, 1 inch = 150 yards.

All these activities doubtless enabled Harris to supplement his already lucrative salary of 100 guineas (enhanced by many other regular payments in the discharge of his other normal duties). Yet it was not a question of profiteering. Howard added:

> Some prisoners, when they are discharged are completely clothed, have a little money in their pockets, and a good character given them, with a further promise that if they bring at the end of the year a certificate from the master with whom they work of a good and sober character, they will be further rewarded.

The bookseller Daniel Prince, whose house lay very close to the castle, was also full of praise in two 1789 letters (printed in John Nichols' *Literary Anecdotes of the Eighteenth Century* in 1812). In July he observed that both new "magnificent" prisons (i.e. the city gaol in Gloucester Green too) were finished, that at the castle being in "a noble style, in imitation of the best old work". In September he wrote:

> The keeper, or governor as he is now styled, is an ingenious architect and mason, and contrives for the good of the publick, and the prisoners themselves, that a great part of the work shall be done by convicts, several of whom, by their industry and manifest reformation, have obtained their release at the expiration of two instead of three years.

It was fortunate for Harris that the 1790s was a relatively peaceful time in terms of international relations, a short breathing space between the ill-fated American campaign and the Napoleonic wars to come. It was also a time of much-improved methods of policing, inspired by the example set by the Fielding brothers' instigation of the Bow Street Runners in London.[*]

---

[*] Not that Harris' years in charge were completely without incident. There were 16 executions at the castle between 1787 and 1809, including the notorious cases of Thomas White (1787), who was brazen enough to steal from the Duke of Marlborough at Blenheim, and Thomas "Oxford Tom" Smith, Charles Evans Shury, John Castle, James Williams, and Giles Freeman Covington (1790 and 1791), whose fascinating story is told in *The Abingdon Waterturnpike Murder*.

Some excerpts from *Jackson's* reveal the relative calm prevalent in Oxfordshire at the time. On 1 July 1792, for instance, there is mention of what was called a "maiden assize" (meaning one with no capital convictions), with only two prisoners' cases heard. In January 1793 only three cases of felony were heard at the quarter sessions, and even those were for petty offences, prompting the newspaper to comment that "for some time past the gaol has been remarkably thin of prisoners, which must be chiefly attributed to the excellence of the county police, and the very diligence of the magistrates". The compliment was repeated a year later, when the small number of prisoners was again noted at sessions in which only three prisoners were tried (and all acquitted). On 3 May 1794, *Jackson's* reported a surely unprecedented occurrence, there being

> not a single prisoner now under confinement for any felony whatsoever. This affords additional proof, if any was required, of the very excellent police establishment in this county, which has been so frequently urged by the judges of assize as an example to other counties.

This "police establishment" was still amateur and largely parish-based, it should be noted; but the Oxfordshire authorities did, it would seem, give greater support and encouragement to the individuals undertaking this role than elsewhere. Consequently, Oxfordshire was still leading the way in 1796: *Jackson's* commented on 9 April that the "the excellent police within the county" was the reason why only two prisoners had appeared at the assizes, and none at all at the quarter sessions, while in "every neighbouring county the prisoners for trial much exceeded the usual number".

However restful this state of affairs was for Harris, the consequent reduction in available manpower did mean that the all-in service that he had earlier been able to offer on the Oxford Canal and River Thames was no longer so easily achieved. But in any case, at the castle itself there was still plenty to occupy him and the men under his charge, and some chance discoveries opened another avenue for his multiple talents – archaeology. Harris would no doubt have had his appetite for the subject whetted by the discovery of a stone coffin in 1789, recorded in *Jackson's* of 18 July 1789 as being "under the old wall of our castle nearly contiguous to the Great Tower, and within about 3 feet of the surface. In this coffin was a compleat human skeleton with this remarkable circumstance, that the skull was placed upon the bones of the feet". The internal shape of the coffin, it was suggested, meant that "the head had been severed from the trunk before interment".*

It was almost inevitable in the course of such major redevelopment of a site with so many centuries of occupation that unexpected subterranean discoveries would be made. (The same thing has happened during the recent wholesale commercial redevelopment of the site.) Intrigued by some of Harris' discoveries, a historian called Edward King explored the site with him in 1794, and found the results so exciting that he felt compelled to publish the initial findings in advance of his intended schedule. The result was *Vestiges of Oxford Castle* (1796), in which many of the plans and illustrations were drawn by Harris (see FIGURES 3, 9, and 10).

King gave ample praise to Harris' contribution, noting that his "inde-fatigable labours ... and skill as an architect and builder has enabled him to search out every part with minuteness". In so doing, Harris also delved into parts of the site which were not disturbed by the building work, and made new discoveries on the Castle Mound. Most notably he investigated the vaulted chamber at the top, and discovered

> in the floor of the room, a circular opening, four feet in diameter ... walled up after the manner of a well, and filled with rough stone and rubbish, amongst which were found horses bones, dogs bones, and three or four horse shoes, and at a depth of about twenty feet, several human skeletons.

---

* Harris would also have been aware that when John Howard had visited Oxford in 1777, Solomon Wisdom had mentioned that when building "a little hovel, and digging up stones for the purpose from the ruins of the court, which was formerly in the castle, he found under them a complete skeleton with light chains on the legs". Howard had surmised that these were probably the remains of "a malefactor who died in court of the distemper at the *Black Assizes*", a thought also aired by *Jackson's* at the time: the issue of 21 March 1767 stated that the skeleton had been uncovered when "removing some ground in our castle green eastwards of the ruins of the old County Hall, memorable as the place wherein was held the fatal Black Assize in the year 1577" (see Chapter Four).

FIGURE 9: A drawing of St George's Tower by Daniel Harris for Edward King's *Vestiges of Oxford Castle* (1796). Work is only just beginning on the task of building up the walls, suggesting it was drawn some years earlier. The buildings in the background would seem to be in Tidmarsh Lane (called "Titmouse" in Davis' map on page 21).

FIGURE 10: The well room on top of the castle mound and the crypt near St George's Tower, drawn by Daniel Harris for Edward King's *Vestiges of Oxford Castle* (1796).

King also credited Harris with the discovery of the foundations of two three-foot thick walls, evidence of the conjectured Norman hexagonal stone keep, and also what King deemed to be "a curious little Saxon crypt" near St George's Tower. Harris had been obliged to alter its internal structure – although only after recording the original arrangement with his unfailing draftsman's precision (see FIGURE 10).

So Daniel Harris, it will be appreciated, was not your average prison governor. As such he was allowed considerable freedom by the magistrates, who knew a good thing when they had one. A man able to offer such a wide range of skills as well as keeping things in order was so very different from his predecessors that they went to considerable lengths to retain his services. In 1808, his salary was nearly doubled to £200 "exclusive of an allowance of thirty pounds per annum for coals and candles". In addition Harris was to be paid £200 "out of the county stock as a remuneration for past services done in superintending the buildings of the castle gaol, and for an increase of his salary from the time of his first applying for the same". At the same Trinity sessions, however, Harris was given a mild reprimand in respect of his two turnkeys, whose weekly pay was raised to 15 shillings. This was presumably in acknowledgement of their additional responsibilities on account of Harris' frequent absences, since it was made clear that "it is the duty of the gaoler to give that situation his entire, regular and uninterrupted service". The multi-talented Harris was obviously prone to letting his attention wander from his main responsibility as governor. The pay-rise was a final ploy to get him to concentrate on the basics of the job. It failed. Harris resigned the next year to pursue commercially what was evidently his real passion of architectural design.* The departure of this remarkable man marks

---

* Harris did not entirely forsake his prison connections. When his replacement, John Wyatt, completed his service in 1823, the next governor was Thomas Dilly, who was married to Harris' youngest daughter, Elizabeth (1801–1829). Harris had three other daughters with Susanna Tompkins (1765?–1822), the daughter of an eminent Oxford grocer, whom he married in 1789. These were: Susanna (1791–1835), Mary (1797–1889), and Martha (1799–1864?). Mary Harris married John Barnard from Sawbridgeworth (in Hertfordshire) in 1827. Daniel Harris died at his home in New Road, from where he could see daily the prison to which he had contributed so much, in June 1840.

the end of a momentous era in the history of Oxford Castle Prison. Genealogical details of the men and women who ran the establishment over this period remain frustratingly elusive. More can often be discovered about the prisoners for whom they were responsible, however, and the following chapters will reveal the stories of some of the more exceptional men and women whose periods of incarceration was overseen by Harris, the Wisdoms, the Ettys, or their predecessors.

CHAPTER TWO

ESCAPES, EVASIONS, AND "ENLARGEMENTS"

The resources available to the criminal justice authorities of the eighteenth century were limited. Crime detection depended mainly on the abilities and enthusiasm of parish constables, untrained and often ill-suited individuals of varying degrees of commitment, elected on an annual basis. More prominent figures such as a coroner, the keeper of the nearest prison, or even the local justice of the peace might become involved if the gravity of the crime warranted it, but generally it was the individual parish which bore the brunt of the burden. Wealthier landowners often took the law into their own hands, and there are many examples of men with the necessary finances, influence, and time pursuing successful prosecutions through their own efforts.

Minor cases were decided at the local petty sessions, and more serious offences at the quarter sessions, held every three months or so, in the presence of local justices of the peace who had a working knowledge of the law. More serious felonies, normally including any for which a capital conviction was possible, were heard at the assizes, held in Oxford every January and July, in front of senior judges engaged on a regular circuit of the county towns of several contiguous counties. The venue for the petty and quarter sessions was the Guildhall (on the site of the current Town

Hall in St Aldate's). The assizes were held at the Shire Hall (or Sessions House) within the castle complex (see FIGURES 2 and 3) until the Black Assize of 1577, but after that, with occasional exceptions, at the Guildhall until a new County Hall was opened in New Road (on the site of the ancient Shire Hall) in 1841.[*]

For the free-spirited individuals who typically found themselves behind bars, incarceration – even under reasonably civilised conditions – would have been a difficult thing to bear. As John Howard expressed it in a 1784 *Appendix to The State of the Prisons in England and Wales*:

> Convicts are generally stout, robust young men who have been accustomed to free diet, tolerable lodgings, and vigorous exercise. These are ironed, and thrust into close, offensive dungeons, some of them without straw or other bedding, in which they continue, in winter fifteen or sixteen hours out of twenty four, in utter inactivity, and immersed in the noxious effluvia of their own bodies.

Such conditions could be better tolerated if there was at least some sense of how long they would have to be endured – even if that did mean eventual transportation to an uncertain fate in an unknown land. With the prospect of even that unpredictable destiny removed in 1775, however, with the outbreak of the American war, one can sympathise with those men and women who felt a compelling desperation to escape. This chapter mentions some of the more ingenious, daring, or plain foolhardy episodes over a period of ten or so years until the rebuilding of the prison made escape almost, but not quite, impossible.

Escaping was one thing, however; staying undetected was another. It is not clear from all the cases reported just how many got clean away, or indeed, what fate befell those who did. Certainly the evidence suggests

---

[*] G.V. Cox, in *Recollections of Oxford*, recalled of the 1790s: "I remember when the Town Hall, in which (in those hanging days) two or three poor creatures had been condemned in the morning to be hung for horse or sheep stealing, was hastily and tastefully *got up* for a County ball in the evening! – to be turned into a Court, at both ends, next morning!!"

that almost all were re-arrested, with a stiffer penalty the usual result of their efforts. In conditions of limited mobility (the population being constrained by the parish poor laws into remaining within or close to their parish of birth or domicile), no escaped convict could remain unsuspected for long close to home. Other options – grasped by many of the individuals featured in this book – were to adopt an alias elsewhere in the country, to enlist in the military or navy, or, more commonly, to seek anonymity in the sprawling, ill-regulated suburbs of London. A high proportion of the criminal acts recorded in this book had some connection with London, either as the destination for stolen goods, or as the home base of perpetrators of crimes on Oxfordshire soil, or as a place of refuge. It is for this reason that Sir John Fielding's increasingly efficient Bow Street Runners make occasional and telling contributions.

The maxim "crime doesn't pay" is as selectively true today as it has always been. But for those men and women whose arrest or re-arrest warranted a reward, their exploits did at least provide them with an immortality of a kind often denied those whose deeds were far more notorious and widely publicised at the time. This lasting fame comes in the form of descriptions printed in *Jackson's Oxford Journal*. The purpose was both to alert the public and to offer a reward, one of the most effective stratagems available to the hard-pressed and largely amateur enforcers of eighteenth-century justice. These descriptions do more than simply help modern readers to visualise the individual in question. Occasionally a place of birth is mentioned, providing a clue for family historians, and students of fashion will find the descriptions of clothing of interest. At a time when few people could afford more than the clothes they stood up in, attire was a highly distinguishing feature. Finally, because Jackson's often devoted considerable space to the mode of escape, some interesting details about the extent and function of the castle buildings also emerge.

The Empress Matilda

✦✦✦

For the most famous flight from Oxford Castle we need to go back almost one thousand years, however, to the turbulent times of King Stephen's reign. It was not an escape made by a prisoner in the normal sense of the word. The Empress Matilda (or Maud) was the daughter of William the Conqueror's second son, Henry I, and although she was indeed a captive in the castle, she was there with many of her supporters, besieged by Stephen, who was also a grandchild of William. In contesting the right to the throne, the two cousins brought England to a state of civil war, known as The Anarchy. The situation came to a head in 1142, when Stephen's forces surrounded Oxford Castle, which Matilda had adopted as her headquarters in the previous year, when Robert d'Oyley (the second, nephew of the original custodian) threw in his lot with her. After three months the situation had become critical. Matilda knew she must surrender or flee. She chose the latter option. Her escape one snowy December night set a precedent for cunning which has never been emulated. Clad in vestments of snow-white invisibility, she and three knights were able to cross the frozen River Thames undetected by Stephen's surrounding forces. Making her way to the safety of Abingdon, then Wallingford, Matilda was able ultimately to ensure that her son would be crowned Henry II.*

---

* Henry II succeeded his uncle, Stephen, in 1154. Probably most infamous for his part in the murder of the Archbishop of Canterbury, Thomas à Becket, in the Oxford context Henry is most conspicuous for his adulterous affair with Rosamund Clifford, honoured through time as "Rosamund the Fair" (whose final resting place was Godstow Nunnery, to the north of Oxford – described in *A Towpath Walk In Oxford*). His two sons (and future sovereigns), Richard ("the Lionheart") and John, were both born in Oxford, though not in the castle, which Henry declined to use as a royal residence.

"Black Bess" and her children

Matilda made her daring getaway in 1142. No doubt there were many other escapes from Oxford Castle over the next six centuries, but the absence of records means that few can be identified. One escape which is verifiable, however, is of another woman. The story of the memorably named Betty Bing, alias "Black Bess", demonstrates the dilemma of the authorities when dealing with mothers who had no means of support. The evidence is patchy, but within the bills that the gaoler (probably Marmaduke Etty) submitted over a period of six years, a little of her intriguing story can be pieced together. The earliest bill is for her "lying in" (or "groaning", as childbirth was also referred to), and for nursing her child for 26 weeks to the 12 July 1726. Whether this was for the newborn child, or an existing one, is unclear, since the next quarter contained a bill for a midwife to attend her at the assizes in July, and for treating her child for measles.[*]

The considerable cost of providing food and clothes for "Betty Bing's child" was as regular a payment as any made by the County over the next few years. Yet costs relating to Bing herself were avoided – at least until early 1729 when the County again met the expense of a midwife and nurse, along with "bread, cheese, ale, and fire" during her labour, plus "blankets, clouts, coats, shoes, stockings, frocks and food". In the bill for the next quarter, therefore, the charge is for two of Bing's children and herself – although the newborn child died after only a few weeks (to be buried at St Thomas' on 3 February 1729). The regular payments for the

---

[*] Bing's crime and sentence remain undiscovered, unless she is one and the same as Elizabeth Hughes (or Hews), who was brought to the castle on the 24 June 1726, according the Calendar of Prisoners for Trinity 1726 (one of only a few to survive from this period), charged with stealing a horse near Chipping Norton. Also known as "Black Bess", Hughes was given the death penalty for the crime, commuted to 14 years' transportation, and it is just possible that Elizabeth Bing and Elizabeth Hughes are the same "Black Bess". If so, the sentence of transportation was presumably impossible with a small child to consider, so both would have had to remain at the castle.

older child continued unabated for another four years or so, the last being in early 1733, when the child must have been at least five years old.

Just these bare facts are intriguing enough. Why did the County, uniquely it would seem, maintain Bing's presumably illegitimate child for so very long, but contributed almost nothing for Bing herself? Was she present in the castle the whole time? How and by whom did she fall pregnant for a second time? What does the sobriquet "Black Bess" imply? Yet to add further mystique, Bing absconded in the latter part of 1729, seemingly abandoning her child to its fate. It is not clear if she succeeded – there are no further references to her, only to her child – but she had a good go! To add to all the other expenses relating to her, therefore, the County was now obliged to repair two locks and pay a mason who spent "four days work in building up the wall where the door was broke by Black Bess and her accomplices … endeavouring to make her escape". The gratitude of some people!*

The proportion of *Jackson's* four pages which covered local news each week was very small, and usually devoted to domestic announcements of births, deaths, and marriages, the weather, and local politics. Criminal acts often rated a mention; escapes from prison always did. It can therefore be taken as a reliable guide that no-one at all found the means to elude William Wisdom's care from the newspaper's launch in 1753 until 1773, as the first such mention came in September 1774.

---

* Bing's case raises the possibility that she invoked what was dubbed "benefit of the belly". This dictated that a pregnant woman should not be hanged, on the basis that the embryo was an innocent party. In theory, this only delayed the sentence until after the child was born, but more often than not the mother was ultimately spared as well. This loophole is said to have created a uniquely male form of employment, that of "child-getter", whereby if a woman was not actually pregnant when she went inside prison, she would do her best, given the lethargic workings of the law, to be so by the time of sentencing! One of the more salacious rumours about Oxfordshire's most notorious patricide, Mary Blandy, sentenced to hang in 1751 (see Chapter Five), was that she had been made pregnant by one of William Wisdom's sons.

A brothel-keeper and a deer-poacher

-+->-<+-

The man in question was Edward Clarke, 25, a former servant of Worcester College, who had been charged with keeping a disorderly house, in other words a brothel, in Friars Entry (near Gloucester Green). He escaped by scaling the wall of the castle on the 13 September 1774. Charles Wisdom, in one of his final acts as gaoler, advertised a reward for Clarke's capture, advising that he was five feet tall, with a "smooth face, fresh complexion, picked nose, hazle eyes, and dark brown hair" and that he was wearing "a fustian frock and waistcoat and leather breeches". Two months later, a 40-year-old shoemaker called William Ward followed suit. This time it was the newly appointed Solomon Wisdom who provided the details, describing Ward as a former gentleman's servant from Charlbury who was "5 foot 6 inches high, fair complexion, light brown curled hair inclined to grey ... sniffs with his nose often when he talks". He was wearing a "blue coat and waistcoat with yellow buttons, fustian breeches with a small stripe or rib, a small hat bound and partly cocked with hooks and eyes". Finally, making one marvel that he got away at all, "he has a large rupture, which he endeavours to conceal by frequently holding his coat over the part".

Rewards of five guineas were offered in both instances. Clarke was subsequently retaken, and made to stand in the pillory for one hour on a Saturday in November (see box overleaf). It is not clear what happened to Ward. He too had suffered in the pillory in his home town of Charlbury for stealing deer in 1768, and is presumably the same William Ward of Charlbury, called then a higgler (or pedlar), who was convicted of the same offence in 1769, and of felling wood unlawfully in 1771.

When he issued the description of William Ward, Solomon Wisdom probably thought it was a one-off, as escapes had been so rare in his predecessors' experience. He was wrong: he would issue many more "Wanted" notices in the following 12 years in charge. As mentioned in the preceding chapter, this was probably as much to do with the sudden overcrowding caused by the cessation of transportation to the American colonies and the dilapidation of the buildings as it was to Wisdom's inability to supervise those inside them. The following incidents show the problems he was faced with.

THE PILLORY was a form of justice often favoured for its immediacy in cases where public ridicule was considered an appropriate punishment – for dishonest tradesmen, slanderers, and homosexuals, for instance. It provided the public with both entertainment and a warning, but had uncertain results – occasionally even fatal ones. In Oxford the pillory was almost always positioned in Cornmarket, where the victim was totally at the mercy of a mob who could choose to throw anything from rotten tomatoes to heavy stones. Hence, it was well worth taking a little trouble to win over a potentially hostile crowd, a line taken to good effect by William Blake in April 1765. Convicted like Edward Clarke of keeping a disorderly house (in St Giles), Blake was brought up from the castle, and put in the pillory at about 11 o'clock one Saturday morning. With uncharacteristic jocularity, *Jackson's* of 27 April 1765 described how, under the watchful eye of "a messenger of the Castle", Mr Blake "upon mounting the rostrum … very judiciously bespoke the favour of the populace by a harangue to the following purport:- 'Gemmen, I hope nobody will millest me as I don't stand here neither for theft, nor murder, nor for suicide, nor sodomitical practices, nor yet for wronging no-body.' This pathetic oration had the desired effect, and Mr Blake not only stood unmolested, but, as it rained a little, was indulged by being covered with his hat during the great part of the ceremony."

Another eye-witness account of the pillory, from about 1794, was provided by G.V. Cox in *Recollections of Oxford*. Here he said of a man pilloried near Carfax Church that: "The poor wretch (with head and hands projecting through holes in the fabric) was now and then saluted with a rotten egg or some other worse missile. The pillory was a substantial structure, and high enough to expose the sufferer to the view of the jeering crowd."

Breaking out and breaking bones

→►◄←

On 6 May 1780 *Jackson's* reported the escape on 30 April of John Harper, a 20-year-old baker from Woodstock, and three deserters from the Oxfordshire militia, William Helford, William Fawdry, and Richard Wells (33). Harper and Wells had been confined in an apartment in the side of St George's Tower, and

> having found means to break their way through the wall above the door-case in the side of a chimney almost adjoining, got upon the stair case and forced the lock of the Little Dungeon, where the two other deserters were confined. Having done this they likewise forced off a large iron bar which went quite across another door upon the tower stair case, which serving as an iron crow, enabled them to force that door and likewise break through the staircase wall of the tower, about 30 feet from the ground, from whence they let themselves down with ropes.

The chase was on! Harper and Wells "were seen the same day at Bruckin's Weir near Ensham, and again at Coate, near Bampton, where a farmer hid them under some straw". The farmer's motive is unclear, but both men could easily have been known to him, as Harper was born in Eynsham and Wells was from Bampton, where he worked as a collar maker. When retaken Harper acknowledged a classic near-miss in revealing that "the hangar with which the straw was probed, in one of the thrusts, grazed against his cheek".* Wells continued into Wiltshire, and helped himself to a horse there on May 9, before returning to his home village of Bampton, where his wife and family lived. Suspicions were evidently aroused, as a recruiting party of marines was sent to the village in disguise soon after, with the result that Wells fell for one of the oldest

---

* hangar = iron hook used for suspending items above ground.

tricks in the book. According to a broadsheet, one of the disguised marines "entered the house where he had secreted himself, and affecting great friendship informed him that there were several people in the town in quest of him, advising him at the same time to make his escape by the back door". There, needless to say, the rest of the marines were lying in wait, and Wells found himself escorted swiftly back to Oxford Castle. He was found guilty of horse- and sheep-stealing, and executed on 30 August. He was said to have been wayward from youth, and a bad father and husband – yet his wife attended him affectionately in prison, and he is quoted as expressing regret "that his wife and children would be twitted with his misfortune". He had been a bell-ringer in Bampton, and asked that when "his corpse arrived there, the bells might be muffled, and that his companions might honour his memory with a dumb peal".*

A similar escape was reported in *Jackson's* of 15 September 1781. Unfortunately for James Eldridge, a deserter, Richard Geden (of St Thomas' parish), and Nicholas Hemmings, it was also reported by a large number of people in the neighbourhood as it happened! It was 7pm and still light when the three men broke out "by forcing the door of the felons' hall, and breaking through the tower stair case about 10 feet above the ground from whence they let themselves down by tying together the sheets from their beds". Only Eldridge avoided recapture, the unfortunate Geden breaking his leg in the attempt.† He was buried, as Richard Guiden, at St Thomas' Church on 12 June 1783, after what can only have been a very unpleasant 21 months.

---

* Wells was baptised at Bampton on 24 October 1746, and married Rose Stone on 26 August 1777. The very next day, Rose, under the name Wells, was back in church to baptise her daughter, Elizabeth. Both are named as parents of a daughter, Rose, christened on 27 March 1779, however.

† Geden had been the apparent victim of an assault earlier that year "with the intent to commit an unnatural crime" by Richard Tarrant. Tarrant was sentenced at the quarter sessions in May to be whipped, and charged a £50 fine and two years' imprisonment (*Jackson's* 2 June 1781). But Geden himself was then brought in the following month charged with committing "a most odious crime" with Tarrant the previous January. Geden then received the same sentence of two years in prison for "sodomitical practices" and "during that time to be thrice severely whipped" (*Jackson's* 28 July 1781).

Thomas Hilborne: a bigamist and a brawler

→►◄←

Escapes were all too often doomed to ultimate failure. In the case of an Oxford victualler called Thomas Hilborne, it was the escaper himself who was doomed, making his attempt surely the least successful ever. Poor Hilborne had had an eventful year. In *Jackson's* of 4 February 1775 he was obliged to apologise for his assault and ill-treatment of Mr William Prickett of Oxford, yet the same week was committed to the castle for another assault in Magpie Lane (just off the High Street). At the March Assizes he was sentenced to six months in the castle for this and for helping one Eleanor Jackson to escape from the city bridewell (by this time on the castle site). Hilborne's own botched escape was described in *Jackson's* of 10 June 1775. Described as a "resolute fellow", he had tried to escape before,

> having at one time nearly cut his way through the wall of the dungeon; at another almost forced a window frame on the north side of the prison; and at another perforated the wall of the room over the gate-way in order to fix a rope whereby he might scale the outer wall.

Prior to this, his final and fatal attempt, he had placed a small bet with another prisoner as to the height of the tower, in order to gauge the length of rope he might need. It proved to be 75 feet, but Hilborne had only been able to acquire a length of 60 feet, which in any case broke eight or nine feet from the top as he made his way down. It was daylight, and his fall was seen. When help arrived, he was still "quite sensible, but his limbs were so dreadfully fractured, and he had received so much internal injury, that he expired in about an hour". It later turned out that his desperation to escape was driven by more than his fear of the sentences for his Oxford misdemeanours. He had also been charged with a capital felony in Somerset, and was a bigamist, and therefore saw escape as his only chance.

"A very artful defence":
Joseph Simmonds and some
"most daring as well as turbulent offenders"

→>⤛+

It is intriguing to learn that the clichéd image of prisoners escaping from castle towers by shinning down ropes or ladders made of sheets has some basis in fact. But prisoners found other uses for sheets too: Thomas Haddon used his to effect an "escape" of a more permanent and drastic nature. Haddon (presumably the same as was baptised in Charlbury on 24 February 1763) had been arrested for robbing the Banbury Mail outside the Kings Arms at Deddington in February 1782 with William Holmden, a marine who had been in Oxford as part of a recruiting party. Holmden was traced in Portsmouth, and later "admitted King's evidence" (i.e. turned informer). Haddon was traced at Warwick, and duly condemned to death at the Oxford Assizes of July 1782. But before the sentence could be carried out, *Jackson's* informed its readers, he found the means to hang himself from an iron bar in the window of the condemned cell "by tearing the sheets of his bed and fastening them to his garters". As was common practice with suicides, his body was interred in the public highway, in this case the Botley Turnpike Road, "without coffin, tho' he had provided one previously". It is indicative of the dread with which dissection was held that Haddon's friends, "as soon as the body was thrown into the grave, ripped open his belly, and filled it up with unslaked lime, to prevent its being taken up for dissection". The body of an executed highwayman Isaac Darkin (see Chapter Five) had been subjected to the same drastic attention in 1761.

Haddon was part of a large network of Oxfordshire criminals. Two others brought in on Holmden's evidence were Joseph Simmonds, keeper of some livery stables in George Lane, and his servant Paul Ragg. After the robbery at Deddington, Haddon and Holmden had ridden to Oxford where Simmonds and Ragg helped to burn the incriminating evidence of the mail bag and its unwanted contents. The authorities were quickly on to them, and although Haddon and Holmden had already departed, Simmonds was surprised in bed. Joseph Simmonds was a resourceful character, however, as the tale of his next few years will show. Surprised or not, he escaped barefoot across Gloucester Green, and hid in a house opposite Worcester College "by getting a considerable way up the chimney, and from whence he refused to come down till he was threatened to be fired on". A subsequent search of Simmonds' house in George Lane revealed a large cock and hen, stolen the previous night from The Catherine Wheel at Sandford. Now alerted to more than just the Banbury Mail robbery, the authorities expanded the search. At his farmstead in Wallingford, Simmonds' brother, Robert, was found to have two copper tanks stolen from the empty house of the late Mr Phillips of Magdalen parish and 30 sheep skins belonging to Mr Richings and taken from a piece of garden ground near the castle.

By June 1782, two more of the gang found themselves contemplating the inside of Oxford Castle. Holmden had thrown light on another unsolved crime involving the Simmonds brothers and Ragg, with the result that two Oxford labourers, James Slatford and William Best, were summoned to explain their part in it. All five men were implicated in the burglary of the house of Mrs Fredericks in Bampton in the previous January. The gang had been interrupted when a servant girl managed to slip out and raise the alarm, causing the men to make a hurried departure. Later a distinctive piece of evidence was discovered at the scene – Best's hat. The extraordinary reward of £50 immediately offered by Mrs Fredericks for apprehension of the thieves was matched by the residents of Bampton, reflecting a general desperation among rural communities in conventional methods of detection.

And there all six men (including the doomed Haddon) remained, awaiting their fates. Despite the evidence of that incriminating headgear, the Fredericks burglary was not proven against any of them at the March 1783 Assizes. Instead, Slatford (then 36), Best (33), Ragg (38), and Joseph

Simmonds (29) were found guilty of burgling the house of Mrs Griffiths (or Griffen) at the foot of Christ Church hill more than a year previously. For this all four were given sentences of seven years' transportation to Africa (the west coast being a destination to which, it was hoped, a small number of transports could still be sent). That there is no further mention of Robert Simmonds (32) rather suggests that he, like Holmden, turned informant.[*]

Joseph Simmonds was not a man to sit on his heels, and on 17 July 1783 he added escape from the castle to his earlier unsuccessful foray not-quite-far-enough up that neighbouring chimney. This action, and Solomon Wisdom's inevitable subsequent notice, gives us a visual image of the former mercer's apprentice, as 5'6" tall with "hazle eyes, thin smooth pale face, brown curling hair, a small mole on his left cheek" and "several boils, particularly one under his chin". Best accompanied Simmonds in his flight over the wall of the debtors' yard. He was described as a 5'7" timber sawyer of 33, who had been born in Oxford. He had "grey eyes, but has lost the sight of the right eye, brown straight hair, thin face, pale complexion". Both men were deemed by Wisdom to have a "sallow countenance from sickness".

Best was recaptured at Botley within a couple of weeks. At the next assizes, in March 1784, his seven years' sentence of transportation was changed to death on account of "being found at large in this kingdom without any lawful cause before the expiration of the term for which he was ordered to be transported to Africa". This was a common charge levelled at apprehended escapees, consistently preferred to any additional charge of actual escape from custody. Nonetheless, the death penalty was only rarely invoked for physically able young men involved in unaggravated theft, and Best's sentence was commuted to transportation for life.

Best may have failed to enjoy his liberty for long, but Simmonds was made of sterner stuff, and it was not until October 1783 that he was traced.

---

[*] It is feasible that Robert was the unnamed brother involved in Joseph's later re-capture in London, with its hint of a set-up. The parish records of St Mary's in Wallingford reveal that Robert was baptised on 5 June 1751 and Joseph on 16 April 1753, showing how much caution is needed with the ages in the Calendar of Prisoners, where Robert was stated as being 27.

JAMES SLATFORD AND WILLIAM BEST. By April 1784, Joseph Simmonds' comrades had all been removed (William Best for life, Paul Ragg and James Slatford both for seven years) for onward passage to Africa. They departed among a total of 22 convicts dispatched from the castle in March (see Chapter Three). The story of Best and Slatford had a later sequel, when *Jackson's* reported on 18 March 1786 that "the widow of the notorious Best, lately transported from this place, has declared on her death bed, in the presence of the minister of her parish, that her husband and Slatford, another person transported from this city … were the persons who robbed Mrs Dunn, laundress of St Peter le Bailey" a few years earlier.

Slatford and Best were notorious and habitual offenders. Slatford had already served two years in prison for an unprovoked attack reported in *Jackson's* of 2 March 1776. Mr Joseph Martin of Stanton St John was one of a party of pigeon shooters who happened to be drinking in the King's Mill when Slatford threatened to denounce the landlord for selling beer without a licence. "He was repeatedly desired to go about his business, but instead of complying, he took out a large knife, and swore he would stab the first man that molested him." That unlucky man was Martin, who was stabbed in the groin "though not so effectually as to be attended with any fatal consequence".

Then in February 1780 Slatford and Best were summoned (but later discharged) on suspicion of stealing "a large quantity of plate and divers other things from the Knife Hole in Magdalen College … and from the pantry belonging to the common room at Christ Church".

Another curious public reference to these two men occurred in December 1774, when Best placed an announcement denying rumours that he had committed an indecent act on Edward Meysey, a yeoman of Waterperry. The fact that he, Slatford, and one John Crofter had been seen drinking with Meysey at The Bell Inn at Wheatley had given rise to the "greatly injurious" aspersions.

Even then, it took an elaborate scheme to trap this wily character, involving the collaboration of the Oxford and London authorities. Thus it was that John Smith (the keeper of the Oxford City Gaol) and a constable, Richard Spindlove, succeeded in luring Simmonds and his brother (unnamed, but probably Robert) to join them for supper at a Westminster hostelry. During the meal, four officers from Bow Street pounced, among them Mr Jealous and Mr Clarke (who feature elsewhere in successful arrests on behalf of the Oxfordshire authorities), and Simmonds was taken back to Oxford. This time he was held in the lower dungeon "from whence …", *Jackson's* reported with satisfaction on 25 October 1783, "… it may be presumed, no small difficulty will attend any future attempts for an enlargement".

Simmonds' spirit cannot be doubted, whatever his other shortcomings; nor can his popularity among his peers, who connived in at least two other of his attempts to avoid justice. On 20 December 1783, *Jackson's* reported the discovery that Simmonds' fetters had been weakened using a tool made by "forming about three inches of that part of a case knife next the handle into a kind of chisel, probably carried thither in the mouth [sic] of some of the prisoners." Pewter had been used to disguise this handiwork, in anticipation of breaking out after inspection, but the ploy was detected.

Simmonds' final attempt, a desperate last throw of the dice only days before his hearing (at the Easter Quarter Sessions, for some reason, rather than the March Assizes), was reported in *Jackson's* of 17 April 1784. Again, outside help was apparent, as Simmonds' wife had

> found means to convey into our castle a couple of back files, in a clean shirt, sent to one [Thomas] Owen, a locksmith, one of the capital convicts reprieved at our late assizes, and being also possessed of two strong clasp knives, for saws, the felons found means to cut away the thin bars placed before the dungeon window to prevent any attempt upon the strong ones behind. Having thus far succeeded, and Simmonds having administered an oath of secrecy (upon his prayer-book) to each of his companions, the night

following was to have covered their enlargement. But on Thursday morning, upon their being unlocked at the usual hour, William Furnell alias Cherry, another reprieved convict, gave information to the keeper, who seized the implements, and it has since been found requisite to chain those most daring as well as turbulent offenders, by night, to the floor of the dungeon in which they are confined.

Simmonds received the death penalty at his hearing a few days later. Technically, as for Best, this was "for having been found at large in this kingdom before the expiration of the term for which he had been sentenced to be transported". The spirited Simmonds made what *Jackson's* called "a very artful defence", however, and his sentence, again like Best, was commuted to life banishment. It was another eight months or so before he took his final departure, given the lack of transportation ships at this time, and he was taken first to Woolwich to be held on a hulk called *Censor* (*Jackson's* 8 January 1785). Three other prisoners accompanied Simmonds on his travels. Two were John Hawkins and William "Bumper" Smith, both of Oxford, the latter being the only man noted as having successfully escaped from the castle only to turn himself in again.

A gang of Oxford burglars

➤➤◄◄

William Smith and John Hawkins were transported for a crime committed exactly a year earlier, when they had effected a burglary which *Jackson's* recounted in rather greater detail than most in its issue of 31 January 1784. The break-in had occurred at the premises of an Oxford grocer, Mr Isaac Lawrence. Hawkins and his brother Richard were known offenders, and when they were observed to be spending freely the same evening at a public house in George Lane, in the company of Smith, another Oxford labourer called Edward Ladds, and "some girls of the town" suspicions were raised. When they were visited the next day, money was found stashed at the Hawkins' lodgings in St Thomas' parish, and John Hawkins was seen to give his brother a small box which "he found means to throw into the river". It was recovered, however, and found to be the snuff box that had been stolen from Lawrence's premises, along with £37, some earrings, some port, and some cheese. Smith and Ladds had sniffed danger, and tried to flee, but got only a mile or so before being apprehended at Medley House, on the Berkshire side of the Thames near Binsey. There Ladds immediately confessed, saying his role had merely been to stand watch while John Hawkins and Smith entered the premises, "lighting themselves by a burner taken of one of the lamps near the place".

Ladds was shown leniency for his candour and minor role, and Richard Hawkins' involvement had been merely incidental, so only John Hawkins and Smith faced trial at the quarter sessions in April. Their initial death penalties were subsequently commuted to transportation to America for life for Hawkins, and ultimately 14 years in Africa for Smith. When the latter escaped, an unusual double reward was offered in a notice in *Jackson's* of 17 July 1784. Solomon Wisdom offered the customary five guineas for information leading to Smith's arrest, or ten guineas for anyone who actually apprehended him. Uniquely, as far as can be told, the same amount was offered in addition by Richard Tawney on behalf of the Oxford Corporation. Smith, who had been born in St Peter-le-Bailey parish, very close to the castle, was described as being 5'9" or 5'10" tall, and aged about 22, with "dark grey eyes, strait dark hair, fresh complexion, stout made … has sores upon both his legs, and had on a blue coat, green and white waistcoat, and long trowsers". The notice was unnecessary, and the rewards unclaimed. Within a fortnight of his escape, as *Jackson's* related on 24 July 1784, he "surrendered himself by knocking at the castle gate and requesting to be re-admitted to his old apartments".

Elizabeth Boswell and the unwise Wisdom

The social status of these eighteenth-century escapees stands in some contrast to that twelfth-century pioneer of Oxford Castle escapes, the Empress Matilda. She remains as the most famous, but a woman from a very different background should surely rate a close second, as the only person known to have escaped from the castle *twice*! For Elizabeth Boswell (alias Mason) was a humble Gypsy, born at Long Sutton (near Abingdon) in about 1756. Her story surfaces in May 1775, when she was arrested with her common-law husband, a tinker called James Corbett, for stealing goods from John Hitchcock's shop in Beckley. Corbett was executed at Oxford on 14 August 1775, claiming, it was said, to be "happy in being prevented from committing further depredations upon the publick". Boswell, though expressing a desire to share the same fate, was instead given a sentence of 14 years' transportation. At the time, August 1775, this was just about still feasible, although delays and uncertainty were inevitable, as the American situation was assessed.

In the second edition of *The State of the Prisons in England and Wales*, John Howard observed that the women's night-room in 1780 measured only 6½ feet by 4 feet. For a woman accustomed to the freedom of a travelling Gypsy's outdoor life, confinement in a space little bigger than a coffin must have been hard for Boswell, especially as she succumbed to the dreaded contagion of smallpox and required nursing for the best part of a month. She had not long recovered when she made her first escape, in October 1776, by which time she had already been held for well over a year. One can imagine the embarrassment of the superbly (but on this evidence, inaccurately!) named Solomon Wisdom that he had allowed possibly the first clean escape of a female prisoner from Oxford Castle for more than 600 years; so much the worse for him that the second prisoner to escape that day was also a woman! They had outside assistance, according to *Jackson's*, gaining their liberty "through one of the windows adjoining the road, assisted, as it is supposed, by some of their accomplices, who cut out the iron bars, by the help of a ladder and drew them through the breach". The episode is made all the remarkable because the second woman, Rebecca Hall, was "big with child" at the time. It is indicative of the small physical stature of people of the period that though she was described as "stout made" she was able to squeeze her pregnant belly through a gap measuring only 17" by 12" to gain her liberty.*

Solomon Wisdom duly issued descriptions of the two women. Ten guineas' reward was offered for Boswell, "about twenty years of age, stout made, about five feet seven inches high, dark eyes, long brown hair, if not cut, fresh complexion, rather hangs her head down in her walk". Hall (who was born in Buscot, Berkshire, in about 1755) rated only five guineas, and was "five feet five or six inches high, brown eyes, light brown hair, some of her teeth out before on the upper part of her mouth, fair complexion".

Not surprisingly in view of the distinguishing feature of her pregnancy, Hall was the first to be traced. She was returned to the castle and delivered of her child in December or January. Nursing during four weeks of "lying in" cost 36 shillings, with an additional 10s 6d each for the services of a manmidwife and apothecary, Anthony Rawlins, for two weeks, and a nurse for the same length of time. Further costs were lodged for maintaining her and her child for another 27 weeks, at 7 shillings a week, during which time she faced trial at the March 1777 Assizes, with what result is not known. By the autumn, her name had vanished from the records.

Elizabeth Boswell's case too was heard at the same March Assizes. She had been recaptured at Tetsworth in February and conveyed to Oxford in a post-chaise, the owner of which duly received from Solomon Wisdom the reward of ten guineas. As is apparent from the verdicts handed down to escapees such as "Bumper" Smith and Joseph Simmonds, eluding custody before the period of transportation had ended (or even begun!)

---

* Hall was in prison for stealing "two silver spoons, several pieces of bacon, wearing apparel and divers other goods" from the dwelling house of Dorothy Bailes of Piddington (*Jackson's* 29 June 1776).

carried a capital penalty. Perhaps Boswell was sincere in wishing to follow her partner Corbett to the grave, because, on receiving a reprieve, rather than show contrition, she instead showed Solomon Wisdom a clean pair of heels for a second time! She had to wait almost another year, during which she succumbed again to sickness, requiring 15 weeks of nursing, but in February 1778 the opportunity was contrived in this "most artful and long-premeditated" way, as *Jackson's* called it on 7 February 1778.

Boswell, seemingly feigning an ailment on this occasion, was alone in the "sick apartment" while two highwaymen Robert Thacker and John Jones (alias Jefferson) and four others were in the condemned cell, "which is secured with two doors, the outer of which had a strong lock and two bolts, the inner two bolts". Thacker had sawn through the staple on both the single lock on the sick apartment door and the one on the condemned cell door, and then disguised his handiwork with cement. Boswell was thus able to break out in the early evening and release the two men. They then secured the doors again, cut their fetters, and

> forced their way through the side of the tower, upon a level with the high wall on the west side of the felons' yard, from thence by the help of the sheets from their beds, they let themselves down, over the iron spikes, into a garden adjoining the castle ditch, and got clear off.

Solomon Wisdom offered rewards of five guineas each for Thacker and Jones, but only two guineas on this occasion for Boswell. Jones was about 24, five feet two or three inches tall, with "large grey eyes, hooked nose, swarthy complexion, long visage, is strait made, speaks thick and short, with dark hair, tied". His exploits had been described in some detail in *Jackson's* of 8 March 1777. He had stopped the Birmingham Fly (an express passenger service) about three miles from Tetsworth on Milton Common. Most highwaymen had the wit to make themselves scarce once the deed was done; Jones decided to chance his luck with a repeat performance on a coach called the Diligence later the same morning. It was not a smart move. Tetsworth was presumably already astir after one incident of daylight robbery, and the driver of the Diligence had no difficulty in persuading two armed men to return with him in pursuit. They got their man, but not without a struggle. Jones, "upon being called upon to surrender … presented a pistol at one of the men, and threatened to blow his brains out, upon which without further ceremony the other fired his gun loaded with duck shot and dismounted the highwayman, wounding both him and his horse". Jones was found to have on him "a pair of pistols loaded with powder, a pair of bullet moulds, a spare flint, a crape hatband, a book of the roads with a leaf doubled down at the road upon which he then was, and 36 shillings in silver with some halfpence". Within the quarter sessions documentation is a surgeon's bill for "attending John Jones, a felon who was wounded in the head and arms". The surgeon did what some might have considered an unnecessarily good job, because Jones was sufficiently recovered from his wounds one month later to attempt to escape.[*]

Robert Thacker, the other man to escape with Jones and Boswell in February 1778, was

> about twenty-four years of age, 5 feet 7 inches high, by trade a taylor, was formerly a bridewell-boy at Black-friers, with strait brown hair; had, when he went away, a false tail, which might be tied on occasionally; hazle eyes, hooked nose, thick lips, high cheek bones, smooth face, strait made, and has a sore leg.

He had been imprisoned since October 1777, arrested with Richard Latham for stopping a coach at the "six-miles stone" on the Maidenhead

---

[*] Jones was one of five prisoners whose attempted escape was detected in April 1777. One of the others was Peter le Maitre (see Chapter Three). Using faggot sticks and a holdfast from the pump, the men had gradually undermined a wall in the felons' apartment where there was a drain which had formerly been a doorway. They disposed of the spoil down "the necessary". Their plan was discovered when one of the mats which covered the hole was moved, revealing tell-tale signs of daylight. They had since been handcuffed and more closely confined (*Jackson's* 5 April 1777). This was not the only time the "necessary" played a part in an attempted escape. In June 1782, with timing which suggests the influence of Joseph Simmonds and his cronies, "a couple of new spring saws in frames, tied and sealed in brown paper" were found there, and an intended escape foiled. This success was ascribed by *Jackson's* to "the vigilance of Mr Wisdom" (*Jackson's* 15 June 1782).

to Henley road. There had been eight people in the coach, but only two – Richard Taylor, landlord of The Bear Inn at Henley, who was deprived of his silver watch, and Bett Cox, who handed over half a guinea and a nutmeg grater – appear to have lost anything of value. At the time, *Jackson's* described Thacker and Latham as "notorious offenders", who had been active in London and elsewhere the preceding three months.[*]

On escaping on 1 February, Elizabeth Boswell, John Jones, and Robert Thacker stuck together initially, although on this her second bid for freedom, Boswell remained at liberty for less than a month. *Jackson's* of 28 February 1778 reported her return, conveyed to the castle by a young gentleman who apprehended her near Wantage. The report included an update on the whereabouts of Jones and Thacker, as disclosed by Boswell herself. The three had stayed at a public house in Faringdon the previous Tuesday and slept under a haystack near Wantage the following night. Boswell divulged that the two men had changed their clothes and hair styles – Thacker having tied his hair with a false tail, while Jones had pinned his hair in curls – yet the second reward notice published by Solomon Wisdom, rather sloppily, one would have thought, repeated exactly the same descriptions as three weeks earlier (see FIGURE 11).

As usual, the fugitives found that they had no place to hide. The bill submitted to the magistrates by Solomon Wisdom in relation to their arrests (see FIGURE 12) shows they tried to hide rather farther away than many, however. Initial search parties were sent to various places, including Deddington and North Aston, as well as London. Boswell having been located, further searches were made for Thacker at Harrow-on-the-Hill (specifically at The Cross Keys), but it was the men employed by the Bow Street magistrate Sir John Fielding who again came up trumps, escorting

---

[*] Thacker and Latham too had attempted an earlier "enlargement" from Oxford Castle. Four spring saws and a crowbar had been sent down from London by one or other's wife. These were "conveyed through a grate over the mill adjoining to the tower in which they were secured", but an accomplice failing to appear, the tools were returned unused and taken to a local inn. There they were discovered, in the first ever such reference in *Jackson's*, "through the vigilance and uncommon assiduity of Sir John Fielding" (*Jackson's* 13 December 1777). Latham was later executed at Reading, in March 1778.

OXFORD CASTLE.

WHEREAS on Sunday Night laſt, the 1ſt of February, 1778, the three following Priſoners found Means to make their Eſcape, by breaking through the Wall of the Tower, viz.

ROBERT THACKER, committed for a Highway Robbery, done near Maidenhead Thicket. He is about twenty-four Years of Age, 5 Feet 7 Inches high, by Trade a Taylor, was formerly a Bridewell-Boy at Black-Friers, with ſtrait brown Hair; had, when he went away, a falſe Tail, wl i'h might be tied on occaſionally; hazle Eyes, hooked Noſe, thick Lips, high Check Bones, ſmooth Face, ſtrait made, and has a ſore Leg.

JOHN JONES, alias JEFFERSON, condemned March 5th, 1777, but reprieved. He is about twenty-four Years of Age, 5 Feet 2 or 3 Inches high; large grey Eyes, hooked Noſe, ſwarthy Complexion, long Viſage, is ſtrait made, ſpeaks thick and ſhort, with dark Hair, tied.

ELIZABETH BOSWELL, alias MASON, aged about twenty-three Years, a tall and ſtout-made Woman, born at Sutton, near Abingdon, Berks; freſh Complexion, light brown Hair parted before, hazle Eyes, a ſtrolling Gypſey, under Sentence of Tranſportation.

FIVE GUINEAS Reward for each of the Men, and Two GUINEAS for the Woman, will be paid on their being delivered to the ſaid Goal, by me,

SOLOMON WISDOM, Keeper.

FIGURE 11: *(above)* The notice placed by Solomon Wisdom in *Jackson's Oxford Journal* of 7 February 1778, following the escape of Robert Thacker, John Jones, and Elizabeth Boswell.

FIGURE 12: *(opposite)* Solomon's Wisdom's bill for the pursuit of Jones, Thacker, and Boswell, and the arrest of the latter. The cost includes a guinea for "Sir John Fielding's clerk to advertise in the London papers".
[*Copyright: Oxfordshire County Record Office*]

Expences occasioned by prisoners breaking Gaol & escaping Feby 1.st
in the night 1778

	£	s	d
The Keeper with a Guard to London on Monday Feby 2.^d in pursuit of the prisoners paid the hire of two horses for 3 days	2	2	0
paid Mr Bond Sir John Fieldings Clerk to advertise in the London papers	1	1	0
expences on on the Journey	3	0	0
sending to several places different parties in pursuit ..	10	0	0
The Keeper with a Guard on Information of the prisoners lurking about Deddington & North Aston & two horses 3 day	1	10	0
paying the Guard & expences	2	2	0
paid the reward of bringing Elizabeth Boswell otherwise Mason to Goal Feby 26.th 1778	2	2	0
on Information of the prisoner Eliz: Boswell, that Jones and Thacker being at the Cross keys kept by a Mrs Kemp Harrow on the Hill paid the hire of post Chaise	7	0	0
paid a Guard with arms	0	5	0
Turnpikes and other expence	0	15	0
paid Simmons carriage to London & back	0	10	0
by who oath the person of Thacker was Identified before Sir John Fielding paid Simmons for his time	0	10	0
paid Mr Jackson the printer for advertisements _ _ _	30	17	0
	1	16	0
Thackers account the reward _ _ _ _ _ _ _	5	5	0
Sir John Fieldings Men bringing the prisoner to Goal	3	2	6
paid their expences returning to London _ _ _	3	10	0
	44	17	6

Allow Mr Wisdom Fifteen Guineas
in part of the above Note to be paid by the
County
                    Chris.^r Willoughby Chairman.

Thacker back to Oxford, from where he was transferred to Reading to stand trial in July 1778. The total bill for the capture of Boswell and Thacker came to the considerable sum of £44 17s 6d, including the cost of sending someone to London to make a positive identification of Thacker. Jones, whose capture is not included in Wisdom's account, was ultimately, after a series of respites from a capital conviction, sentenced to "hard labour on the Thames", as too eventually was Thacker. Elizabeth Boswell's ultimate fate is unknown. In summary, this determined woman was held at the castle from May 1775 to October 1776, then February 1777 to February 1778. Her third spell lasted at least another year, as she was still present, and still requiring the services of a nurse, in the summer of 1779. After that, however, her name appears no more.

William Hanks:
a jaunty and bare-faced thief
-->--<--

It is difficult to assess the preceding incidents, observed briefly and imperfectly over two centuries after the fact. The true motives and natures of these escapees can only be guessed at. Admiration, sympathy, and distaste are aroused in approximately equal measure. However, it should be noted that every one of these "enlargements" occurred before the major building works of the 1780s. So the one escape known to have occurred after this makes its perpetrator all the more remarkable. William Hanks, from Hanborough, was obviously among the most determined and athletic of those people known to have successfully eluded the castle's hold. Sadly for his chances of leisurely enjoyment of his triumph, though, he was also among the most imprudent!

Hanks had been arrested for stealing cloth, gold, and silver from the Reverend Mr Friend, the Principal of New Inn Hall, and also of taking a watch from the house of Mr Samuel Denton of All Saints. He was inconvenienced for only a matter of days. On 20 August 1793, he contrived an escape "from the felons building … by breaking through the grating that encloses the day room", and thence scaled "the boundary wall towards the Castle Mills, and got from thence through an adjoining garden". A notice in *Jackson's* of 24 August offered a reward of ten guineas above the statutory amount. Hanks (22) was described as 5 feet 5½ inches tall (the specification of the half inch being, perhaps, indicative of Daniel Harris' fastidious engineer's eye!), "well made, fresh complexion, hazle eyes, brown hair" and was wearing "a light coloured coat, striped waistcoat, buckskin breeches, worsted stockings, and a round hat", giving him the "appearance of a groom". A second otherwise identical notice a week later added a further reward of five guineas. This was offered by John Smith, keeper of the city gaol, who was at pains to point out that it was he who had apprehended Hanks initially, but that the prisoner had been the responsibility of the county authorities at the time of his escape. This is the only known time when anyone eluded the clutches of the castle while Daniel Harris was in charge. Smith's comment might be read to imply negligence, but on the contrary, even here Harris manages comes out of it with credit. In making a payment to him of £19 5s 6d "for apprehending and retaking" William Hanks, the magistrates commented that the "escape was not effected through any negligence of the said Daniel Harris, but on the contrary that the said Mr Harris had taken every precaution for the security of the said William Hanks".

It took Harris less than a month to retrieve his man. In some respects, it is surprising that it took so long, because Hanks had made scant effort to cover his tracks. He had swiftly found service at Woodstock, and had the nerve to show his face in Oxford on several occasions. Indeed, he had taken an early coach into Oxford on the day of his re-arrest, eaten breakfast at The Cross Inn (also called The Golden Cross, in Cornmarket), then taken the Worcester coach back to Woodstock. But someone there had finally recognised him. His obvious bravado very nearly carried him through, when "he called himself Smith, and so boldly confronted those who challenged his person that for a while they became rather doubtful of his identity", as *Jackson's* put it on 16 September 1793. Only the arrival of John Smith, a man who really could identify him, settled the matter. Hanks was removed to Botany Bay in Australia for seven years in the following May.

It is easy to warm to a resourceful, audacious, but seemingly ingenuous character like William Hanks, who, given half a chance, one suspects, would have adapted well to the untried opportunities of a new life under Australian skies. We may never know how he fared – nor the fates of those hundreds of others whose stay in Oxford Castle was a prelude to a long trip on a transportation vessel, and a rather longer stint of hard labour at the end of the voyage. But we do know some of the reasons why people found themselves in this predicament in the first place, and the following chapter outlines but a few of the more interesting examples.

CHAPTER THREE

HARD LABOUR:
"AT HOME" AND ABROAD

The systematic transportation of criminals to the colonies of the West Indies or America became established in the 1660s. There was a temporary lull in the 1680s, when merchants perceived the shipping of slaves from Africa as a more profitable cargo, but early in 1718 an act was passed, which standardised the sentences and made this home-grown human cargo a more viable option. With few exceptions, criminals guilty of non-capital offences received seven years' hard labour overseas; those reprieved from capital crimes received 14 years; anyone detected on British soil before the expiration of either sentence received life. Given the very large number of offences for which the death penalty could be allocated – over 200 by the beginning of the nineteenth century – this produced a very regular supply of candidates, as judges tended to apply leniency whenever the opportunity arose. The first stirrings of revolt against British rule in America occurred in April 1775, meaning that destinations such as Maryland, Virginia, and Georgia became very soon out of the question. For a few years, Nova Scotia and unspecified parts of Africa were considered a possibility for a few, but for all the others who would otherwise have faced a period of forced labour over-seas, their destination became no more exotic than Woolwich. The first transportation ship to Australia sailed early in 1788, but it was several years before this distant and untried destination could confidently accept the large numbers of miscreants that the "Old Country" was still so very keen to be rid of.

Hard labour across the Atlantic

→>-<←

The earliest quarter sessions reference to the transportation of any Oxfordshire prisoners appears in the Calendar of Prisoners for 5 April 1687. Three men – John Carter, a miller from Shipton (for burglary), Peter Beer (for stealing a basket of linen), and William White of Benson – are noted as facing this sentence, and later that year a fourth man, also called William White, had joined them, charged with stealing a horse.* Next year, on 15 August 1688, the gaoler (presumably Robert Thorpe) was ordered to deliver Carter and the two Whites, plus Thomas Webster (transported for horse theft) to John Langborne, keeper of Gloucester Gaol, "who hath undertaken to transport them". All had been removed from the castle by May 1689.

This is the pattern of evidence on which this chapter is based: a record of the sentence in the Calendars of Prisoners, the issue of an official order to transport from the under-sheriff of the county, the bill submitted by the gaoler for conveyance to the ship, and the subsequent absence of the prisoner's name in the castle records. It is evidence which is not conclusive. The documentation is incomplete, and it should be noted that simply because an official order was made for a person's transportation, it does not necessarily follow that he or she actually made the journey, nor survived the voyage. Each case of transportation needed

---

* All were no doubt among the "poore prisoners in the castle … forced to undergo greate want and suffer great calamities", whose "humble petition" was heard by the magistrates at the quarter sessions of Michaelmas 1687.

the authorisation of the Secretary of State before the Oxfordshire Under-sheriff could prepare his orders. There might then be a further delay while a suitable ship was located. Many prisoners, as with the first three mentioned above, might already have spent many months in prison, during which it is possible that some might have escaped, or died, or been reprieved before physical relocation was possible. What became of Beer, for instance, whose costs had been paid, yet was missing from the Calendar of Prisoners by Michaelmas 1688, well before the others were moved, is unclear. And how intriguing that the earliest positive identification of transportation from Oxfordshire should include two men with the same name!

It appears that no further instances of transportation from Oxford occurred until late 1694, when John Jeffreys and Robert Smyth (both of Nettlebed) along with James Platt (all condemned for horse theft) were removed, assuming that their request to enlist in the army as an alternative failed. Henry James of Bampton (for highway robbery), and the first known female transport, Elizabeth Norton of Deddington, followed in 1695.

The next two references are, unusually, to individuals who had *already* been removed. A comment on the prisoners' bread bill for Michaelmas 1700 stated that Edward Franklin and John Woolhams had been transported on 7 September 1700. Franklin, of Horspath, had stolen some "bees and howes [hoes]" belonging to Richard Goswell of Temple Cowley, and the widow Mary Brown's ladder in 1697. Unrepentant, he erred again in 1699, this time finding that stealing oats from Edward Ford of Garsington was sufficient to earn banishment to the colonies.

At Easter that same year of 1700, Mr Etty (presumably Andrew) had been ordered to remind the justices at the next session to pay Long-borne, the Gloucester gaoler, for having already transported old John Staite. It is worthy of comment that Staite (also styled Stayte and Steat) was defined as "old". There was a logical tendency to show leniency to older men, especially those with families. The motive was not necessarily compassionate – if a transported man left behind him a family, he would leave hungry mouths to forever burden the Poor Rate. And of course the plantations needed fit, young individuals, able to contribute their full quota of effort and stand a better chance of surviving the journey. Staite was a habitual offender, having already experienced confinement in the castle in 1690 for clipping coins and in 1696 for burglary. His third offence, taking £16-worth of gold and silver from the house of Elisabeth Dobson of Aston Rowant in 1698, earned him the death penalty, commuted to transportation.

Staite was the last transport to leave verifiably via Gloucester, probably for onward delivery to Bristol. In the 1720s, transports from Oxford were taken to Bristol direct. In the quarter sessions documentation for Easter 1723 there is a bond for £200 issued on 7 December 1722 to a Bristol merchant called Jonathan Becher (and witnessed by Marmaduke Etty). Of the ten people named, four were not actually from Oxfordshire, although they had committed their felonies on Oxfordshire soil. The others were Thomas Lowe (a butcher from Bampton), Sarah Cooke (spinster of Burford), Thomas Pickmore (a labourer from Oxford), Richard Waine (a stonecutter from Milton), and John Trentham (a butcher from Deddington). All had been found guilty of grand larceny, and therefore by this time faced specific sentences of seven years. The tenth prisoner, Richard Cooper, an Oxford labourer sentenced to 14 years for burglary, had pleaded "benefit of clergy" – a late instance of this centuries-old means by which influential members of society eluded the justice meted out to the less privileged.* The contract stated that Becher must acquire a certificate of delivery from the governor or chief customs officer of the colony within four months of the date of the bond, and present it to the Oxford Clerk of the Peace within a year to receive payment. It appears

---

* "Benefit of clergy" had originated as a means by which churchmen could avoid the justice of a lay court. A reduced punishment was imposed on any accused person who could read the opening verse of the 51st Psalm. Initially this ability was almost exclusively the preserve of the clergy, but the term stuck when its scope was widened, so that by about 1550 it was applied to anyone who could read, an educated mind being one which was incapable of malevolent deeds, it would seem! The flaw was that people could claim leniency simply by memorising the words. The practice was accordingly officially abandoned in 1706, although the phrase (and test) continued to be used as a means of avoiding the common punishment of branding on the hand for petty thefts.

to be the only example of such a contract retained in the Oxfordshire records, but all others presumably contained similar stipulations.

Further orders for transportation occurred erratically until about 1730, with groups of convicts conveyed every few years, seemingly always via London from 1724 onwards. From 1737 until 1776, when the practice ceased, the exodus was on a near-annual basis. Almost without exception, the crime which earned these people such severe punishment was theft – very often of the most trivial nature. James Norford had been found guilty merely some handkerchiefs in 1747, for instance, and Richard Dyer of stealing peas in 1758. But perhaps the most pathetic case of all was that of Robert Eaton whose crime in 1757 was to steal some mere rags.

Among the near 300 people for whom transportation orders were made to leave Oxford between 1697 and 1775 some were from the same family, compounding no doubt the trauma for those they left behind. The two William Whites may have been the first such; two men called Bailey were also surely related, convicted of the same crime of stealing shoes in Burford in 1737. In 1758 came the first obvious occurrence of a father and son, John Crook(e) senior and junior, both being ordered for transportation for a theft at Wallingford. A few years later, a father and son named Thomas Gulliver followed suit, albeit on separate vessels.* Both had originally been committed together on 8 October 1760 for the theft of some shirts at Fringford. The younger Gulliver was sentenced to seven years at the March 1761 Assizes, but his father was discharged. It was a temporary reprieve. Both belonged to what *Jackson's Oxford Journal* called "the Bicester gang", the full extent of whose activities was revealed by the King's evidence provided by one of their members, Joseph Westbury, in December 1762. As a result of his revelations about the "iniquitous practices of this nest of villains", six men were charged with 18 robberies committed over the previous few years. Gulliver was one of the six, and followed in his son's wake early in 1763, on the particular charge of stealing

---

* These two were probably either Thomas the son of Edward who was baptised on 1 April 1711, or the son of Richard, baptised 10 November 1725. The younger Thomas was baptised on 25 September 1747, his parents (Thomas and Mary) having married on 5 July 1747 (all at Bicester).

peas at Stoke Lyne. Westbury was discharged, care having been taken meanwhile to keep him separate from the rest of the gang "to prevent them from either tampering with him or doing him an injury".

There were probably more instances of members of the same families transported from Oxford – certainly the same surnames occur too often for that not to be likely – but it is usually not possible to determine the exact relationship. Occasionally *Jackson's* settles any doubts. It exposed the cases of the brothers Charles and James Aris particularly well, for instance. Charles, a former "matross" (a soldier next in rank below the gunner in a train of artillery), had been transported for a theft recorded in *Jackson's* of 2 March 1765, when he stole sheets and other items from the ostler's room of The Star, and similar items from The Wheatsheaf in St Aldate's. He was spotted "marching off with his plunder in a sack", at which point he dumped his haul and "took to his heels". Pursued with a cry of "Stop Thief!", he found himself in a cul-de-sac, so "made a double in the chace … and meeting his pursuers, pleaded his innocence" – to no avail. He was taken thence to the city gaol, then the castle, and subsequently, in the spring of 1765, rather farther afield – albeit not for long. On 14 June 1766, *Jackson's* reported that Charles, or "Cagey" as he was called, had "already finished his travels", having been spotted "in some of the most public parts" of Oxford. Public indeed, if it was true that "he had the impudence to pay a visit to his brother, now a prisoner in our castle", an act of bravado which led *Jackson's* to suggest – not entirely accurately, as it turned out – that "he will soon find himself under a necessity of paying another visit to the same place".

The sibling in question, James Aris, was described as the brother of the "celebrated" Charles "Cagey" Aris on his arrest in April 1766. He was transported for seven years for stealing iron bars from the palisades of the late Councillor Harris' house. It was James' bad luck that he had not been the first person to have this particular idea, and the house was consequently being watched, with the result that he was caught in the act. Charles was still at large when James was removed, and he was traced only in the November of 1766. At his trial in Reading in March the following year, he was given a respite to allow "for enquiry into the validity of his defence, which was, that the ship in which he was embarked for the plantations was driven out of course by stress of weather, and that himself was forced on shore by the captain". Presumably he was not entirely believed, for he ultimately received a life sentence.

Jackson's is also helpful in identifying possibly the first married couple to be transported – although they did not leave simultaneously. Mary and William Collett were from Enstone. Mary was sentenced to transportation in March 1767 for the theft of a cloak in Witney. She had already experienced a stay in the Witney House of Correction in January 1766, classed as a vagrant for returning to the village of Great Tew from which she had already been once removed. She was accompanied on her travels by John Keen (for stealing a cow) and Samuel Smith (for stealing a sheep), Thomas Hale (for theft of bread in Shipton), and Sarah Cowell (whose seven years' sentence in America arose as a result of escaping from Thame Bridewell). *Jackson's* described their departure "in high spirits" in its issue of 11 April 1767, specifying the crimes of the two women as respectively "stealing wearing apparel" and being "an incorrigible prostitute". A year later, William Collett followed. He had been found guilty of stealing gold rings and a piece of bacon in Enstone; one of the other four people dispatched with him, Hannah (the wife of Robert) White, was found guilty of receiving the stolen items from him. It is tempting to think that Collett (probably the man of that name baptised at Enstone on 24 April 1744) deliberately courted trouble in the hope of being reunited with his wife on the other side of the Atlantic.*

The last order for transportation issued by the Oxfordshire Undersheriff came in the summer of 1776. The convict in question was that arch-escapologist Elizabeth Boswell (encountered in Chapter Two). This

---

* In 1758, another married couple, Richard and Mary Druet(t) or Drewett, had been sentenced to 14 years' transportation for sheep-stealing. The orders for removal were prepared, but Richard died in prison before the sentence could be effected. This couple were probably married at Dorchester on 30 September 1745, when Mary's maiden name is given as Plater. They were soon in trouble, as it is presumably this same newly wed couple, living in Coggs, near Witney, who were accused of theft by Elizabeth Moulder, also of Coggs, in June 1746.

order was not carried out. America had ceased to be a viable destination, and due to her elusiveness, Boswell was still on English soil at least until the summer of 1779. Not that transportation was inevitably a bad thing. For those who survived the voyage and whatever regime and climate awaited them, the New World offered new opportunities impossible to imagine in class-ridden Georgian England.

"Partreg and fesants as plenty as the sparrows be in oxfordshire": David Benfield's letter from Maryland

-->-<--

A remarkable letter from a former Oxford prisoner called David Benfield, written from the "fine and pleasant" environs of Maryland in 1772, demonstrates exactly what a transported man with enterprise might achieve. Benfield had been charged with stealing £40 and a silver tankard from The Crooked Billet in St Thomas' parish. The items belonged to the landlord, Richard Crawford. It wasn't the only thing Crawford lost that day. In reporting the theft, *Jackson's* of 16 June 1770 noted that his wife Mary had also been taken to the city goal for assaulting her husband and threatening his life, he having been "confined by a broken leg, which she had the cruelty to throw out of the box and displace the fractured bones". In the same issue, Crawford acknowledged his wife's elopement, and renounced responsibility for her behaviour or debts. Benfield was sentenced to seven years' transportation in October, having already fallen foul of the authorities a few years earlier for stealing deer from Wychwood Forest, where he had operated as a physician for many years. This was undoubtedly the key to Benfield's subsequent good fortune. A man with even rudimentary medical knowledge possessed a skill much more valuable to the fledgling colony than mere physical labour. Consequently, after his transportation in the summer of 1771, he fared rather better than most.

Addressed to Mr Whitton (David, by then dead in fact), the keeper of the city gaol (or Bocardo), where Benfield had been held for several months, his letter (dated 20 July 1772) outlined his fortunes since his reluctant departure. It was printed in full in *Jackson's* of 5 December 1772 (see FIGURE 13), and mentioned some other former Oxford residents, "worthy characters …", as *Jackson's* ironically called them, "… of whom he makes honourable mention", namely:

- Lucy Bennett, the wife of Tobias, and daughter of a Worcester College butler called Smith. It was for stealing a silver spoon which was part of a much larger haul from the college that Bennett had been transported for seven years, in the summer of 1769.

- Charles Bossom, who had been sentenced to seven years' transportation at the quarter sessions of January 1763 for stealing "diverse pieces of butcher's meat" from Andrew Pearcy of Oxford. Bossom was married with two children at the time of writing.*

- John Brown, sentenced to seven years for stealing fowls in Oxford in 1760, and who Benfield says had married a Dutchwoman, who died, leaving him some land.

- Henry (spelled "Hare") Brown, sentenced to seven years in October 1769 for stealing a fowl from Mrs Chillingworth of Oxford. He had escaped once from the city gaol in March 1770, "in the absence of the gaoler by forcing the keys from his daughter", but to no avail. According to *Jackson's*, Brown, "being betrayed by the clinking of his fetters as he ran through the streets, was retaken near Wadham College".

Benfield provided news of one other person with Oxford connections in "a mericka". But Philip Brickland (probably the brother of William Brickland, a teacher in Catte Street) was there out of choice – and the news was

---

* Bossom is a St Thomas' name inseparable from the history of Oxford's waterways, as too is that of Benfield's victim, Crawford. Another member of the family (whose further exploits are described in *A Towpath Walk In Oxford*), William Bossom, had been ordered for transportation in 1768.

To Mr David Whitton at Bocardo
in the City of Oxford
with Speed   *Ingland*
Boltimore County Melzadys Manner, Mereland

Mr WHITTON

THIS Coms to a quaint you of my well fare and
the good and Bad fortin I have had since I
have been in a mericka I have had very Great Suc-
cefs in My undertakings I have folloed nothing but
phyfick & Surgorey fince I have been heare I have
Don many Good and famus Cures in old wounds I
have Cured a boy that have been Lame for this 10
years and have and Cured many other that have
been lame for 2 or 3 years & have ben under all
the Surgions in this Cuntrey I have Cut 3 Cancers

my power to pay them as soon as the ship Returns
all my old a quaintans Livs neare me but are all
Sarvants which I Dont Ceep cumpany with for I
Keep the beft Cumpany as neare as I Can this yeare
I Shall yearn upwards of a hundred pound I Gives
20 pounds for my bord & horfes hay and Grafs I
find him Corn my self ——————
Let it be fur or neare I allways Charge a Shilling a
mile for My Vifit I have Sent for 40 Miles but 20
often Sir I will Give you a Little a Count of the
Cuntrey the Cuntrey is fine and plefant Cyder uerey
plenty peaches and Chereys as plenty as the haw
bufhis bee in oxfordfhire partreg and fefants as
plenty as the Sparrows be in oxfordfhire all forts
of game are uerey plenty Likewife fifh flefh and
foul Chickins you may by for 2d purpees beef for
3 halfpence & mutton the fame I lives a bout 25
miles from boltimore found and bout 18 from Suf-
quana where Mr. Brickland Told me his brother
philip Lived I have inquired all as I cold and I heare

FIGURE 13: Extracts from David Benfield's totally unpunctuated letter
from Maryland of 20 July 1772, printed in *Jackson's Oxford Journal*
of 5 December 1772.

the Ship belonged to one Iacob Giles was Cold the
Elizabth pleast to Give My Kind Love to all your
brothers and Sisters and My old frind Mr Handrell
and Mrs Bew and Mr Wisdoms and Mr Mears and
Mr Rollins Mrs Gadney and Mrs huse and thair nai-
bor if you pleas that for Sworn Blackgard that Sore
hannah Cripses pillabor which was Marked H C he
Swore the Each was em hee thoat to punish Me
but was mistaken for I Lives Like a Ientleman and
hee Like a blackgard We have had a fine harvest
as fine wheat as Can grow it is sold for 4s & six
pence pur Bushell I shall be uerey Glad to heare
from you to Let me Now how My naibors dos
pleast to Direct for Docter David Benfield to be Left
at Mr Jon Boyds Druggest in Boltimore Mereland
I Conclude with My Kind Love to yon and your
wife and my Little Bedflows Iane peggy and nan-
ney and am your Ever wellwisher to Comand

  ye 20 Iuly 1772   D Benfield
              hare Brown is well &
Charls bossom have got 2 Children and wife Iohn
brown have been married but his wife is Dead he
was Married to a Dutchwomman ho have Left him
a pees of Land Tobacco sels in this Cuntrey for 15
Shilings pur hundred if I had a frind I Cold Ship
Tobacco home but as I hant I Cant makeany thing
of marchandice I have 3 borders at 25 Shilings pur
month all with uerey bad wounds if Lee Elkington
had Com a Long with me hee Might a made him
Self for Ever for heare is Rabits as plenty as they
bee in a warren and make No youse of the Skins a
tall and hats are uerey dear pleast to Give My Love
to Molly Carter & Mrs Bent and Carpenter I Shall
be might Glad to heare what is beCom of Lee I
beg of all Love in the world to Right to me to Let
me now how all my old frinds dos
   I Clude with My harty prayers for you and
am your D Benfield
        Rum is 2 shillings pur gallon
  pray Dont fail Righting pray excuse my Scraul
for I am in hast Luce bennet is a Live and well as
I heve heard but I hant seen She Mike is well hee
is Ceep by the County

less good. He was the captain of a slave ship called the *Elizabeth* and had secured a large number of slaves on a trip "to the islands". He was unlikely to have returned, because, according to Benfield, other "negors roas and got a board and cruely used all the ships cru after whipped them all most to death then hanged them and burnt the ship after releasing all the slaves".*

A number of Benfield's old Oxford acquaintances are also addressed in the letter. These include Whitton's wife, brothers, and sisters, "the Mr Wisdoms" (meaning Charles and Solomon, the county gaolers, presumably), Hannah Cripps (whose property Benfield seems also to have been accused of stealing), and Lee Elkington (an Oxford hatter sentenced to transportation in January 1771, but commuted on account of his youth to serve in the Navy).

Interesting though the names of the Maryland survivors are, it is Benfield's description of his own circumstances and surroundings which must, to an Oxford readership in the midst of winter, have seemed like a wonderland. Beef, mutton, fish, game, chickens, tobacco (which he was thinking of exporting), and rabbits were plentiful, Benfield claimed, and the land produced "as fine a harvest of wheat as can grow". In addition, the cider, peaches, and cherries were "as plenty as the haw bushes bee in Oxfordshire, partreg and fesants as plenty as the sparrows be in Oxfordshire".

Benfield's medical skills undoubtedly made his lot in America much more pleasant than many, and he was probably exaggerating a little, to fan the envy of his former acquaintances. Nonetheless, news of a man who could claim within a year of banishment to reside at Lady Baltimore's Manor and expect to earn some 100 pounds that year was no doubt cheering indeed for any convicts about to make the long journey themselves. Cheering too for Sir John Fielding (of Bow Street), should he ever have heard of it. In 1773 he called transportation "the wisest, because most humane and effectual, punishment we have", on the basis that it

---

* Benfield concludes this chilling news for anyone who knew Brickland with the comment that a slave could fetch 70 or 80 pounds in Maryland – making them a far more profitable cargo than transports, who, with their normally finite period of service, were valued at rather less.

"immediately removes the evil, separates the individual from his abandoned connections, and gives him a fresh opportunity of being a useful member of society". Benfield's was an excellent case in favour of his argument. Not that many Oxford prisoners subsequently had the chance to test Benfield's accuracy. The last major exodus occurred towards the end of 1774, bound for a ship at Bristol again for the first time since 1723, as far as can be told. After that, the stirrings of American rebellion made transportation much less feasible. The usual alternative, for the next decade or so, was to apply forced labour rather closer to home.

Hard labour on the River Thames

The first men sentenced to hard labour specifically on the Thames were the brothers Thomas and William Smith. They had been tried at the assizes of July 1776 for robbing Henry Harrison Esq of Trinity College of nine guineas and a watch on the highway near Witney. As so often happened, they were reprieved from the death penalty, in this case on condition that they apply to enlist for military service in the East Indies, "never more to be at large again in this kingdom". The application was refused, and the rather more convenient sentence of six years' labour on the Thames was applied. Accordingly they were accommodated on board a hulk called the *Justitia* (a former trans-Atlantic transportation vessel) in December. Woolwich, where the *Justitia* (and the *Censor*, another hulk frequently used to accommodate felons from Oxford) lay, was as far afield as many criminals who might otherwise have been transported went for the next few years.

One was the enigmatic Peter le Maitre, one of the most famous of all Oxford Castle's thousands of inmates. His notoriety stemmed from his foreign origins at a time of deep-rooted jingoism, and has given rise to a theory that he was actually Jean Paul Marat (1749–1793), a noted French revolutionary. But no doubt a contributing factor was also the nature of his "victim" – the University's Ashmolean Museum, no less!*

Le Maitre had been in Oxford since at least August 1775, as it was on the 5th of that month that his wife announced in *Jackson's* that her tambour (a newly devised method of embroidery) business had relocated to the Cornmarket. Assuring her customers of unsurpassed "neatness of work and elegancy of pattern", she also offered "lessons in tambour". Her husband, meanwhile, was available to provide tuition in drawing.

When the Ashmolean found itself bereft of numerous golden coins, medals, and chains valued at nearly £200 in February 1776, le Maitre was quickly identified as the culprit, having disposed of some of the items in Oxford before leaving hurriedly for London. From there he made his way to Dublin, using aliases of le Maire and Mara, but was arrested by the Irish authorities and brought back to Oxford in September. It would be six months before the trial, and le Maitre put the time to productive use. In *Jackson's* of 16 November 1776 he announced the first issue of an intended monthly autobiographical publication entitled *The Wanderer and Unfortunate Husband; or the Life, Adventures and Travels of Peter le Maitre*. Claiming to counter the "ridiculous and false" tales then circulating, le Maitre expressed the hope that "the truth will not appear altogether void of charms, nor the adventures he takes upon himself to relate, the less pleasing for being within reach of probability". Subscribers were advised to call at the castle or apply at his house near the back gate to Exeter College, where, presumably, his (equally "unfortunate"?) wife was in residence.

At the trial in March 1777, le Maitre represented himself. The theft had occurred between 3 and 5 February 1776, while he had been entrusted with care of certain exhibits by the curator of the Ashmolean. His defence

* Not the current Ashmolean, but its former home, now the Museum of the History of Science in Broad Street. The same building was used for the anatomisation of corpses, mainly those of executed criminals, until a formal School of Anatomy was opened at Christ Church in 1766/67. Le Maitre's true identity is discussed in two scholarly articles by J.M. Thompson in the *English Historical Review*. These are entitled *The Robbery from the Ashmolean Museum, 1776* (1931) and *Le Maitre, alias Marat* (1934). Marat was responsible for the massacres of many Royalist sympathisers in Paris prisons in 1792, and was murdered himself in 1793.

was that a member of the University had given him the missing items in lieu of a debt. This proving to be false, the judge seemed to take as dim a view of this "horrid insinuation" against a gentleman as he did of the crime itself, and pronounced a sentence of five years' hard labour on the Thames. Consequently le Maitre (and another convict, Thomas Bayliss) were conveyed to a hulk called *Taylor* (or *Tayloe*) on 15 April. Given that it appears to have been almost *de rigeur* to attempt an escape from the castle at this time, it is not surprising to find that this resourceful character had attempted just that in the interim. Four others were implicated in the failed effort, one being the resilient highwayman, John Jones, who evidently treated this experience as practice for his successful break-out of February 1778, a little less than a year later (as described in Chapter Two).

Le Maitre may have escaped the penalty of transportation (and may or may not have reinvented himself as the revolutionary Marat) but by the 1780s, the sentence had again become viable. The news that seeped through from the colonies was by no means all as encouraging as that imparted by the likes of David Benfield. The thought of leaving familiar Oxfordshire people and scenery for a long voyage to strange lands and an uncertain fate must have been terrifying. Most Oxfordshire criminals were unlikely to have seen the sea before, let alone sailed on it. Some sought any opportunity to escape to the last moment. In May 1784, *Jackson's* carried two items in relation to a mass escape from a transportation vessel called *The Great Duke of Tuscany* near Torbay. Seven Oxfordshire criminals were among 25 who were quickly rearrested. These were 55-year-old Richard Wingate (alias "West Country Dick"), Thomas Turner, Edward Harris, William Bowler, Matthew Mills (20), Samuel Hussey, and John Baughan (28), the ages being as per the July 1783 Oxford Calendar of Prisoners. These men were among the 22 whose departure was noted in *Jackson's* of 20 March 1784. Three others were William Best, Paul Ragg, and James Slatford (encountered in Chapter Two).* With over one hundred individuals

---

* Only in the years 1783 and 1784 do the Calendars of Prisoners held at Oxford Castle specify a destination. Ragg, Slatford, and a prisoner called Thomas Jobson (alias Johnson) are consistently noted as destined for Africa (exactly where is not clear), but another nine always for America (presumably Nova Scotia, which remained loyal to the British cause.

from various parts of the country at large, the Devon authorities were stretched to the limit. Consequently, Solomon Wisdom and a turnkey were summoned to Exeter to help with identification.

Hard labour in Oxford

→>-<←

From March 1785, although the sentence of transportation was often recorded against a prisoner's name, this seems consistently to have resulted in rather the opposite. Oxford appears to have woken up to the idea that sending free labour elsewhere, whether it be another continent or 100 miles or so down the Thames, was to its own detriment when there was plenty of work to be done at home – in two senses of the word: "at home" being a cant term among criminals for "in prison".* As the great physical reconstruction of the prison buildings began, who better to provide the labour than the prisoners themselves? Some were obviously so employed until a suitable transportation vessel became available, or until the number of prisoners exceeded the available space, or indeed until the very work they were engaged in compromised their own security. In April 1786, for instance, *Jackson's* stated that three prisoners – among them Thomas Gearing (42) of St Clement's and William Marriner (23), a white-smith of St Peter-in-the-East, accomplices to Miles Ward, who was executed in March 1786 (see Chapter Five) – were conveyed early to a hulk at Woolwich to await a vessel sailing for Africa. This was not because a suitable vessel had been located but because of the insecure nature of the castle gaol, "which is considerably weakened by the demolition of some of the exterior walls, and is now rebuilding with great improvements and upon a very extensive plan".

---

* When the horse-thief James Williams (see Chapter Five and *The Abingdon Waterturnpike Murder*) was tracked down in May 1790, *Jackson's* announced that he had been discovered "in the thieves' phrase, *at home*, being in Clerkenwell prison".

Soon after, Daniel Harris began to exert his considerable influence. Under his assured authority, the practicality of using prison labour became more viable, and references to convicts receiving sentences specifically to undertake "hard labour in the Castle works" became common. The first such were in the Calendar of Prisoners for 7 March 1787. Simultaneously, the enlightened change from seeing prison as a place of actual or impending punishment to regarding it as one of improvement is evident. A fund for establishing "pecuniary rewards to be distributed amongst convicts and prisoners at their discharge, as shall have conducted themselves to the satisfaction" of the magistrates was established. It was funded by subscription, but this was soon unnecessary, as the value of the labour provided by the prisoners proved sufficient in itself. By the end of 1787, the fund had a balance of £113 9s 2d, after all expenses and earnings paid in respect of prisoners engaged in hard labour at the gaol and bridewell, and no further private contributions were requested.

By the end of 1791, the prisoners' efforts "within the walls … on the River Navigation and the repair of the Botley Turnpike road" earned a balance of £115 7s 11d after deducting the costs of their "clothing and maintenance". The comparison was made between this amount and the figure of £122 16s 7d that the County would have paid as bread allowance had the prisoners remained idle. Reporting this in its issue of 18 February 1792, *Jackson's* also took the opportunity to emphasise the wider social benefits, saying

> it is here proper to observe that this mode of recalling the prisoners to habits of labour seems the most rational means of rendering them useful members of society by their future industry, in confirmation of which, several of those already discharged have been since employed in places of some trust, and have hitherto acquitted themselves entirely to the satisfaction of their employers.

It was the same story for at least the next few years, as the demand for labour at the castle, on the Thames and Oxford Canal, and on other

The following statement clearly proves the benefit of the system pursued in the County of Oxford, with respect to the management of the Prisoners under confinement, and sentenced to hard labour. within that County. The number of Prisoners, besides those confined for a short Time, between the 1st of January, 1794, and the 1st of January, 1795, was only nineteen, and the following is a statement of their cost and their earnings : —

	£	s	d
County Allowance of Bread.	35	0	9

N. B. This Expence must have been incurred if the Prisoners had not been employed in hard Labour.

	£	s	d
Extra Food and Clothing,	27	2	8
Overlooker,	23	8	0
Expence in Tools,	3	2	0
Expence of Hire of Horses and Carts on the Botley Road,	3	6	0
	—	—	—
Total Expence,	£91	19	5

	£	s	d
Earnings of Prisoners at the Castle Works,	£78	5	1
Work done on the Canal Navigation,	13	11	0
Done on the River Navigation,	5	14	6
Sawing Stone,	15	10	8
For keeping the Botley Road in repair,	12	12	0
	—	—	—
Total Earnings,	125	13	3
Total Expence,	91	19	5
	—	—	—
Balance,	£33	13	10

It is to be noted, that the Overlooker having so few Convicts to take care of, was almost constantly employed in the respective Works with the Prisoners.

PRICE of STOCKS.

Bank Stock, shut	Long Ann. shut
Five per Cent. 94 ¾	India Stock, ——
Four per Ct. Con. shut	India Bonds, 1 Dif.
Three per Ct. Con. 62 ⅝	Navy and Vict. Bills, 4 Dif.

ADVERTISEMENTS *omitted this Week, will appear in our next.*

FIGURE 14: The earnings and expenses of the prisoners at hard labour at the castle, and on the canal, the river, and the Botley Road, as printed in *Jackson's Oxford Journal* of 28 March 1795.

public works continued unabated (see FIGURE 14). Oxford therefore has much to thank these eighteenth-century felons for – and they were probably thankful themselves, not to be labouring under more exotic conditions. For by 1788 Australia had presented itself as the alternative transportation destination – albeit falteringly for the first few years. The Oxfordshire records are patchy at this point, and provide no firm clues about the removal of men and women to the Southern Hemisphere. There is only one possible instance, in 1808, when Daniel Harris presented a bill for conveying Richard Spittle, Charles Colby, and Ben Jones to a hulk in Langston Harbour, Gosport – but with what precise intention is not clear. This may well have been the sole instance. With so much demand for labour at the castle and elsewhere in Oxford, and an able supervisor in Harris, Oxfordshire may have been unusual in retaining all but its most errant citizens over these latter years. It would be fascinating to discover just how many of the 250 or so men and 30 women known to have been ordered for transportation to America in the 18th century, actually survived, regained their freedom, and, like David Benfield and Charles Bossom, prospered sufficiently to retain the possibility of having descendants alive still today .... .

CHAPTER FOUR

DEBTORS, DONORS, AND DISEASES

The eighteenth-century prisoners in Oxford Castle were consistently identified as either felons or debtors, accommodated in separate parts of the prison. Of the two, in some respects the debtors were worse off, because whereas some provision was made from the county coffers for anyone convicted of a felony, debtors had to fend for themselves. Seven of them petitioned the magistrates in 1727, pointing out that their allowance was only seven farthings (less than two pence) a week while felons received ten and a half pence. In addition, they were locked up for 17 hours every day "some way up the tower in a very cold place which hath caused some of us to be sick", where they were allowed no visitors nor anything to drink. Debtors fell into two categories. Some – enterprising, law-abiding citizens on the whole, no doubt, whose only real crime might have been greed or foolishness – were imprisoned specifically for that civil offence; some, however, were indebted as a direct result of incarceration for some other misdemeanour, finding themselves unable to pay the fine or the accumulated gaoler's fees required to obtain release. Many therefore remained in gaol for inevitably long periods.

The absurdity of this system was highlighted in 1729 by Colonel James Oglethorpe (who became the founder and first governor of the transportation colony of Georgia).* He induced Parliament to enquire into the horrors of the debtors' prisons in London. The practice of farming the prisons out to gaolers whose income depended solely on what could be extracted from the prisoners was standard. This meant that it was not uncommon for a gaoler to torture debtors to death in vain attempts to extract fees from men who by the very nature of their situation had no money to give. There is no evidence that Oxford's debtors received treatment of this kind, although occasional hints do appear of victimisation, deprivation, and possible misappropriation of even the meagre relief which was, in times of dire want, sometimes reluctantly granted. Under these circumstances some men (and debtors almost always were men) spent a very long time indeed inside the castle, with little hope of repaying the debt, and no means of support other than the charity of others.

Debtors' petitions and pleas

→>-<-

THOMAS SALMON:
BAKER OF BICESTER

One common way for a debtor to raise funds was to appeal to neighbours. This is what Thomas Salmon requested permission to do in 1725, in his lawful residence of Bicester. It is not clear how he came to be in that plight, but one suspects from some earlier correspondence that he may have harmed his own bakery business by being just a little too critical of men who had the power to ruin his reputation. In April 1718 he was committed to prison for denouncing four Bicester families as traitors, and

---

* Oglethorpe's Secretary in Georgia for part of 1736 was Charles Wesley (1707–1788). He and his brother John (1703–1791), the founders of the Methodist Church, were greatly concerned for prisoners in Oxford between 1730 and 1735, and taught many to read, wrote their letters, paid their debts, and tried to find them work.

for failing to produce anyone willing to act as surety for his subsequent good behaviour. Early in 1720 he faced further charges on account of a threatening letter sent to Samuel Trotman of Bucknell, the magistrate responsible for his earlier arrest. Salmon, evidently, was a man of many words, not all of them judicious. His letter of January 1725 was much more prudent. He stated that he had already been in prison for 57 weeks, receiving "meagre sustenance" from his wife. Now that too would be denied him as it had "pleased God to visit his family with the smallpox, his house to be fired, his wife burnt and lamed, and his goods to be seized". To add further pathos, Salmon also alluded to the resultant suffering of his three children, the youngest being only 29 weeks old. It is difficult to tell if he succeeded, because of the patchy records relating to debtors, but he did at least survive another decade, to be buried at Bicester on 7 April 1736.

Salmon's incarceration coincided with that of a man whose length of imprisonment made Salmon's seem fleeting in comparison. But then, a very large number of prisoners came to know the name Marshall Tims, because he spent, off and on, the best part of thirty years in the castle!

"AN INCORRIGIBLE ROGUE":
MARSHALL TIMS OF HOOK NORTON

Tims' name first appears in the quarter sessions records of Easter 1722, in a petition for bread, by when he might well already have been there for some time. He had been released by 1724, because he was spotted in September that year carrying a basket containing seven hares, a rabbit, and a bullet mould past the turnpike gate at Yarnton. In April next year, Tims' troubles really began, when he committed an assault on Thomas Freeman of Ditchley (near Charlbury). For failing to pay the resulting fine, he was sent to Witney Bridewell; for failing to resist the temptation to break out of it, he was sentenced to three months at Oxford Castle, commencing early in 1727. In the records for Epiphany 1727, Tims' crime was specified as being "an incorrigible rogue and setting snares in Mixbury warren". But his real problem was his inability to pay his fine, or find anyone willing to commit to a surety that he would keep the peace with Thomas Freeman. You can see why. Somehow he did find the means to engineer his release by the end of 1727, but was soon in trouble for further assaults, on John Minchin of Hook Norton in October 1727 and on Henry Bunting of Cassington in March the next year. Tims, evidently, was a man with a temper, but with no friends willing to vouch for him. It was an unfortunate combination, with the inevitable result that he soon found himself back inside the castle. For two and a half years between Michaelmas 1729 and Trinity 1732 he was detained there "for sureties and to prosecute his traverses". Again he found a means of release, and again he lost little time in re-offending, receiving in 1733 a six-month sentence for shooting at his old adversary John Minchin. The sentence presumably served, he was back again the following year on two counts, a prosecution brought against him by, intriguingly, the Duke of Argyle (for trespass, and not for the first time), and for failure to pay a fine of £10 for a further assault on Henry Bunting. And there, from 1734 on, Tims remained for an incredible further 13 or 14 years. Soon after the summer of 1748 he was finally released.

You might have thought that a man who had spent the best part of 30 years in prison would have learned his lesson, but no, not Tims, who was back inside once more by the October of 1749! What John Dawson of Heythrop (near Enstone) had done to make Tims threaten him "whereby he is in danger of his life" we will probably never know, nor how deserved his very long cumulative period of incarceration was. Clearly, he was not the most convivial of men, and might well have been truly the "incorrigible rogue" that the justices dubbed him, who then fell foul of the law of debt by failing to pay the resultant costs. Many debtors were of a very different ilk, as the many elegantly composed petitions for alms show (see FIGURE 5). Thomas Salmon was a case in point; Thomas Mouldern, a peruke (periwig) maker and barber from Witney, was another.

THOMAS MOULDERN OF WITNEY:
IMPRISONED "NOT FOR DEBT, THEFT NOR DEFRAUD"

Thomas Mouldern's case is illuminated by the opportunity that he took to air his grievances through a medium not available to Thomas Salmon or Marshall Tims: *Jackson's Oxford Journal*. In a series of notices placed in the newspaper between 1776 and 1779, he expressed eloquently the hopeless situation of many debtors, even though his own circumstances were not at all typical. In September 1776, soon after his imprisonment, the 65-year-old Mouldern placed his first notice, claiming that he was in prison solely because an Oxfordshire attorney had cheated him of his rightful estate. Consequently he offered the rights to that estate to anyone able "to avenge his case, free him from prison, and allow him a subsistence for life". There were no takers, presumably, since a similar appeal appeared in the paper in January 1778, reiterating Mouldern's claim to have been wrongfully imprisoned, "not for debt, theft nor defraud", but as a victim of fraud himself. This time he identified Mr John Jones of Wichcombe (sic) as the manipulating attorney in question, and the disputed estate as "Mouldern's Wood" in Ducklington. This, he claimed, "was taken from him by violence after he had been in possession five years". His offer now was a £300 reward for anyone who could help him to prove his birthright and provide charity to help him to survive in the meantime.

Thus far one's sympathy lies with Mouldern, an intelligent man, evidently, with at least a few sympathisers. But two weeks after Jones' name was divulged, *Jackson's* published a response from "Verax" of Witney, which gave another side to the story. Mouldern, it seems, had been given every opportunity to prove in court his right to the estate some years earlier, but had failed to do so. For his failure to pay the resultant costs he had suffered an earlier period of incarceration. When released, Mouldern persisted in cutting down timber in the wood that he so obviously considered to be his own. This obliged the owner to bring an action for damages, and it was this – Mouldern's second failure to pay either compensation or costs – that explained why he was being detained in prison.*

The notices subsequently placed by Mouldern made no further reference to his claim, but concentrated on his own deteriorating circumstances. By July 1779, approaching the end of his third year at the gaol, he had sold all his effects, and was reduced to begging for donations to avoid starving. It did the trick! Half a guinea was contributed, he informed *Jackson's* readers in his next instalment two weeks later, but sadly, as he had had no allowance whatsoever since the end of June, this was insufficient. A further £3 was what he needed "to supercede out of" prison. He concluded: "I humbly beg and pray the charitable and humane to consider my truly miserable and unhappy circumstance, and afford me such relief as they shall think most meet, to help me out of my distress, and I will, as in duty bound, ever pray." Gone was the offer of a lucrative share in a valuable estate; benefactors would have to be content merely with God's blessing now! By October, Mouldern's appeal for charity had attracted the requisite help, including a single gift of three guineas from a unknown lady. Unfortunately, this was still inadequate, he claimed, as he was being prevented from leaving by his opponent's attorney. As a result, Mouldern said, "I have no friend, nor can I help myself, and must inevitably starve without relief, which is what they aim at."

It is difficult to know if Mouldern was a ruthlessly wronged victim, or an obsessive fantasist. Either way, he took his grievances to an unprecedented level of sophistication, and exposed the situation of many debtors with style and conviction. Mouldern was imprisoned at Oxford Castle when John Howard made his early visits. Howard, a man more influential than any in taking up the reforming ideas that Oglethorpe had promoted earlier in the century, had in mind prisoners exactly like Mouldern when campaigning for the abolishment of gaol fees. On his visit to Oxford

---

* In *Jackson's* of 9 May 1772 Mouldern is named amongst debtors intending to take advantage of a new Insolvency Act. He had been held at the castle since at least the summer of 1771. When he was summoned again in 1773, for cutting down 50 oak and 50 hazel trees, the wood was named as Edgely Coppice near Ducklington, and its owner, John Leake Esq.

Castle on Christmas Day 1782, it was apparent that Howard's efforts still fell far short of success. 15 of the 31 felons of both sexes who were crammed into the tiny prison had actually been discharged, but remained as a result of the ludicrous ramifications of a system which required inmates with no source of income to pay their bills before being allowed to leave. The prisoners at Oxford were probably more fortunate than their peers elsewhere in the country, however, in at least being able to benefit from the generosity of the liberal minds and purses that characterised the city.

Charity and "the most expressive effusions of reverence and gratitude"

→>–<–

John Howard described the principal charities existing in Oxford in 1777. Thomas Horde's Charity was the best-established. Horde (as mentioned in Chapter One), "who was confined here for some offence against government, built the chapel" and bequeathed an annual sum of £14 to pay for a chaplain and the same sum for distribution among the prisoners. Horde altered this provision in August 1709 to a legacy of £24 a year to "both forts" (i.e. debtors and felons). But the estates from which this income was derived (one in Oxfordshire, one Berkshire) were able to produce only 33 shillings a month by 1777, "which was paid by the rector of Lincoln College, and is now paid by the principal of Trinity, who are always two of the twelve trustees". The other dual-purpose funds were a somewhat miserly 8s 8d per quarter from Magdalen College, plus 40 shillings every Lent, "commonly called *forfeit-money*", and the following:

> Debtors have in common every Saturday six pounds of mutton sent by a gentleman of Christ church college. From the other colleges they have in bread about 2s a week. Christ church and New college send them both broth, generally three times in a fortnight.

Yet even this came at a price, Howard adding that "the prisoners pay four pence to the man who brings it". That comment immediately raises doubts about how much of these displays of benevolence by concerned Oxford individuals and colleges found its way to its intended beneficiaries. Certainly (as seen in Chapter One), the quarter sessions records are peppered with imploring appeals from desperate inmates. Often they pleaded for food or clothing; occasionally they alleged neglect, but it is difficult to discern much criticism of the keepers of the gaols themselves. That could be because the Oxford gaolers were more humane than many of their counterparts; but it could also represent simple diplomacy. It was very risky to point the finger at someone who could make your life hell – especially if that was what he was already tempted to do! Sometimes the risk was considered worth taking. The debtor David Gadsdon spoke out during the dramatic events leading to the appointment of Daniel Harris in 1786 (see Chapter One), for instance, and in 1763 Thomas Harris, Richard Barton, John Whitton (who was transported in the same year), John Ansell, and Thomas Parry claimed that "the charity money left to the prisoners by Mr Horde has not been paid to us for this thirteen months past". Whether this represented a failure of the trustees or misappropriation by William Wisdom is not clear, but opportunities to cream off alms intended for the prisoners must have existed. The gaolers submitted accounts of the food, nursing, funeral expenses, and other costs incurred for the supposed benefit of the prisoners only every quarter – long enough for an unscrupulous keeper to charge for more than they provided.

And if the gaoler did somehow filter off any alms for his own personal gain, he was not the only one! Sometimes, as in the only reference noted of what sounds like early charity tin-rattling, the money failed even to get that far! It was left to the prisoners themselves to notify the public in *Jackson's* of 11 January 1766 that "two men carrying a poor's box have begged about under pretence of asking charity for us, but no money so collected has been brought, and therefore they must have been impostors".

However, this was an exception, and the pages of *Jackson's* show that help often did reach its intended recipients. In 1773, for instance, something unprecedented happened when a charity set up to provide bread for the poor of the city agreed to allocate its surplus of £3 3s 2d to the Reverend Mr Swinton, the prison chaplain, to buy bread for the prisoners. In the 1780s, numerous notices of appeal and thanks from the prisoners testify to the slowness with which John Howard's recommendations were being implemented. Public thanks was given to Queen's, Oriel, and New Colleges in 1782 and 1783, for instance, and on 3 January 1784, 80 prisoners (26 of whom were debtors) expressed their gratitude to Worcester, Queen's, and Jesus Colleges in addition to many named individuals.

In 1776, the prisoners appear to have taken their fundraising techniques to a more personal level. *Jackson's* of 27 January 1776 mentioned that they had erected in the courtyard "an edifice composed entirely of snow, representing the gothic arch and entrance to a cave". The observation that this "curious construction ... has already attracted the attention of good numbers" suggests that the prisoners had spied an opportunity to seek donations from people who might otherwise have rarely visited the place. No doubt *Jackson's* very mention of it attracted the attention of still more "good numbers" soon after! In fact, over the whole period the newspaper was generally very sympathetic to the unhappy plight of those in the prison, and on 14 February 1784, it took up the prisoners' cause of its own volition, stressing the importance of charitable acts:

> there being no gaol allowance of any kind for the debtors, and bread only for the felons, some of whom, we find, have suffered confinement near two years since their respective trials, notwithstanding the repeated applications of the bench of justices. Hence it will easily be credited that some of them are almost destitute of apparel; to whom any kind of cast-off clothes would be highly acceptable. The keeper we learn has lately been under a necessity of destroying the old matting etc on which the felons slept, in order to relieve them from loathsome vermin, and bed coverings of all kinds are become exceedingly scarce.

Another winter, another appeal. On 11 December 1784 the prisoners, in their own words, requested help "to alleviate their present distressed situation; the prison having no allowance for firing, nor even bread for the debtors, makes it truly a place of a most melancholy aspect". Many debtors were suffering "excruciating misery", while "many of the other prisoners are nearly naked, having neither linen or scarcely any thing to cover them". Again, it had the desired effect. The following week's newspaper expressed satisfaction that all the prisoners had been able to acquire bread, meat, and fuel as a result of benefactions from six individuals, in addition to half a bushel of coals to each prisoner from a surplus raised in the previous winter. Seven more gifts, totalling £16 (including from Lord and Lady Charles Spencer, Magdalen and Trinity Colleges, and William Jackson, the proprietor of the *Journal*, himself), had been donated for future use.

Jackson's recorded other moments of individual generosity too. In 1775, the winner of a large lottery prize, the Reverend John Cox of St Giles, made a gift to be divided among the prisoners at the castle. But then, as he had just won the huge sum of £5,000, he could afford to be generous!

Another clergyman, the Reverend John Swinton (mentioned above), remembered his former charges when he died in 1777, leaving a bequest of £100 from which a sum should

> weekly be laid out in the purchase of bread to be distributed amongst the prisoners in Oxford Castle as should constantly attend divine service, the same to be distributed by the minister attending the said prison, and the keeper of the said prison for the time being allotting to each of them a three-penny loaf till the whole should be expended.

As the century progressed, some attempt was made to provide means by which debtors who met certain conditions might apply for early release. Thomas Mouldern made use of one such in 1772. But if that failed, a debtor either paid his dues or died from want. Unless you happened to be a debtor in late 1786, that is, when something wonderful happened. If debtors often had to rely on help from third parties, so much the better if that third party happened to be the third George!

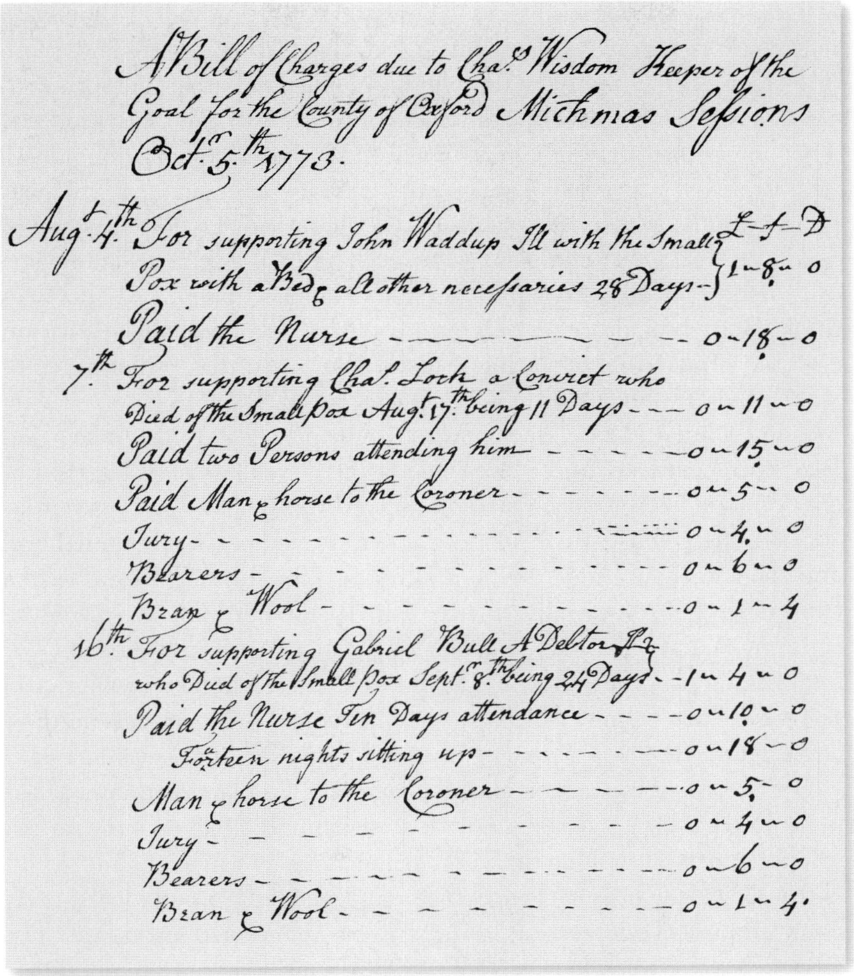

A Bill of Charges due to Chas. Wisdom Keeper of the
Goal for the County of Oxford Michmas Sessions
Oct. 5th 1773.

Augt. 4th. For supporting John Waddup Ill with the Small
Pox with a Bed & all other necessaries 28 Days — 1~8~0

Paid the Nurse — — — — — — — — 0~18~0

7th. For supporting Chas. Lock a Convict who
Died of the Small Pox Augt. 17th being 11 Days — — 0~11~0
Paid two Persons attending him — — — — 0~15~0
Paid Man & horse to the Coroner — — — — 0~5~0
Jury — — — — — — — — — 0~4~0
Bearers — — — — — — — — 0~6~0
Bran & Wool — — — — — — — 0~1~4

16th. For supporting Gabriel Bull A Debtor &c
who Died of the Small Pox Sept. 8th being 24 Days — 1~4~0
Paid the Nurse Ten Days attendance — — — 0~10~0
Fourteen nights sitting up — — — — 0~18~0
Man & horse to the Coroner — — — — 0~5~0
Jury — — — — — — — — 0~4~0
Bearers — — — — — — — 0~6~0
Bran & Wool — — — — — — — 0~1~4

FIGURE 15: Charles Wisdom's bill of Michaelmas 1773 for the costs of nursing some of the many smallpox sufferers of that year, and the funerals of three of them: Charles Lock, a felon due for transportation, and two debtors, Gabriel Bull and Thomas Jones. Lock and Jones were buried at St Thomas' Church.

[*Copyright: Oxfordshire County Record Office*]

Jackson's of 23 September 1786 carried the glad tidings. Following a recent visit to the city, George III had provided £300 to secure the release of as many debtors as were thought deserving. He had also empowered the magistrates to reduce the sentences of any other deserving prisoners. This news, unsurprisingly, was "received by the debtors and prisoners with the most expressive effusions of reverence and gratitude". It was many months before this gratitude was deserved, however, as it was not until April 1787 that the king's benefaction had its effect, enabling 25 of 27 debtors to be freed. Mind you, the Oxford prisoners could perhaps think themselves fortunate that even this long delay was all they had to endure. John Howard, writing in 1789, compared this gift with one of £200 made to the gaoler in Salisbury for an identical purpose. Tacitly praising Daniel Harris, he recorded "with pleasure … this *proper* and *faithful* application of the money" in Oxford, "well knowing that part of the donation to Salisbury was spent for the benefit of the gaoler's tap".

Soon after, charity of this kind was not needed at all. George III had also specifically praised "the plan introduced by the magistrates of the county of Oxford of employing the convicts by hard labour within the castle gaol" during his 1786 visit. Not long after, in April 1787, the fund "for establishing pecuniary rewards to be distributed amongst convicts and prisoners" was created (see page 73). Harris and William Jackson were among those designated to receive subscriptions, the fund being intended "to give every encouragement to the general plan of reform introduced in the said gaol". A footnote said: "It is particularly desired by the magistrates that persons visiting the works of the said gaol will not in future give any money to the prisoners or convicts employed there, as they will receive every proper encouragement from the above mentioned institution."

Which was fine, so long as you were physically able to respond to that "encouragement"…

Death, disease, and disorder

Better treated though Oxford prisoners were compared with many, the castle was nonetheless a place where untimely death occurred on a regular basis, as the insanitary conditions, the poor diet, the lack of air and exercise, and rudimentary medical attention took their toll. Outbreaks of gaol fever or distemper were common, as well as the most-feared killer of all – smallpox. John Howard noted that there had been 11 deaths from smallpox in 1773 alone. Several of these occurred in August and September, entailing a cost for each of 5 shillings to send a man by horse to fetch the coroner, 4 shillings for the jury, 1s 4d for "bran and wool" (for those unable to afford a coffin), and 6 shillings to remove the body, which was buried in St Thomas' churchyard if no other destination was more appropriate. In addition there was the cost of nursing and sustenance, and the coroner's standard charge of £1 plus expenses (see FIGURE 15).

Even with the considerable improvements introduced during Daniel Harris' time as governor, smallpox continued to be a risk. In a letter of 22 June 1790 to the magistrate Christopher Willoughby,* Harris asked for guidance on where he might hold new arrivals, since there had been a recent case among the existing prisoners, which was "an unfortunate circumstance at present as we have so many who have not had it at the gaol". The solution was medical. The following month, according to *Jackson's*, the prisoners were offered inoculations, with the result that "they all experienced the salutary effects which so universally attend this practice".†

---

* Willoughby (1749?–1808) was the magistrate most involved in *The Abingdon Waterturnpike Murder*. He chaired the Oxford Quarter Sessions for more than 20 years, and also led the committee which raised funds for a memorial to John Howard in St Paul's Cathedral. *Jackson's* of 30 April 1791 announced that a total of £1,500 had been realised, of which £200 was to be allocated to prison charities.

† Some prisoners might also have benefited from the presence among their number of the occasional man of science. In a curious reversal of normal practice, a surgeon and apothecary called Hall placed an advert in *Jackson's* of 22 April 1774, offering the public free consultations at the castle, with the request that people "will not be prejudiced against him or his medicines on account of his being so unhappy as to be under confinement".

A prisoner's wellbeing was also dependent on the company he kept. Doubtless it was not always the most congenial. The bill presented by the surgeon John Hawkins for attending the prisoner Stephen Green from 30 May to 2 Aug 1731 was surely not untypical. As a result of "quariling & fighting in the dungeon", Green had ended up with "his hand, arme, and side kicked upon and stamp on in a violent maner", with particular damage to the tendons of his hand "three times lay'd open".

For some, no amount of surgical assistance could help. Prisons were a repository not just for those with criminal intent: they held many people too whose only real "crime" was a disorder of the mind. Marshall Tims might have been in this category; William Lardner (probably from the village of Ramsden) certainly was. Dubbed a "madman", he slit his own throat on 21 January 1721, and needed three people to watch over him until he died five days later – a necessary precaution, probably, as Lardner's violent nature is evidenced by a bill for five shillings for "damage done to a bed … breaking down the bedstead". Another, posthumous, cost of five shillings was for "a woman for washing the bed and bedding which he had bled on". A coroner was called to every death. Often no precise reason was given – the phrase "visitation of God" could cover a large number of ailments, and one wonders if the coroners who regularly pronounced this verdict were conscious of its irony in a place which must surely have seemed as godforsaken as any in Oxford!

Some prisoners' deaths could not be attributed to the conditions, either inside the prison or inside their heads. *Jackson's* recounted the death of an 18-year-old convict called Robert Brox in January 1791, who was accidentally killed while working at the castle when the earth that he and others were moving fell on top of him. There was also a journeyman shoemaker, who, "greatly intoxicated with liquor …", according to *Jackson's*, "… tumbled down from the summit of our Castle Hill, dislocated his neck, and died instantly" in March 1773. But perhaps the most unlucky of all was the unnamed debtor in 1776 who, having been discharged only the day before, was killed instantly when a large stone from the chimney that he was helping to pull down fractured his skull.

THE BLACK ASSIZE OF 6 JULY 1577

Death then has been no stranger to Oxford Castle – least of all after Oxford's infamous Black Assize, when several hundred people died within the space of five weeks. Anthony Wood's account in *History and Antiquities of the University* was taken directly from the register of Merton College, which may have had an especial interest because Rowland Jencks, the man at the centre of the incident, was a bookseller authorised by the University. Jencks was a Roman Catholic of Belgian extraction, whose radical views led to his trial at the assize court of 6 July 1577, held then (but never again) in the old Shire Hall or Sessions House within the castle complex (see FIGURES 2 and 3). The "saucy and foul-mouthed" Jencks failed to convince when he took the stand, and was sentenced to lose his ears. No sooner had the penalty been announced than "there arose such an infectious damp or breath among the people that many there present, to the apprehensions of most men, were then smothered, and others so deeply affected that they lived not many hours after". Six hundred people sickened in Oxford that same day, plus a further 100 who had returned to their homes in outlying villages. Wood described the ensuing weeks for the victims as "very calamitous and full of sorrow, occasioned by the rage of their disease and pain" which caused them to "beat their keepers or nurses, and drive them from their presence. Others like mad men would run about the streets, markets and lanes, and other places. Some again would leap headlong into deep waters."

On 12 August, the contagion ceased as suddenly as it had begun, the death toll having reached 300 in Oxford and 210 elsewhere. The victims included most of the magistrates, including the sheriff, Sir Robert D'Oyley (a relative, though not direct descendant, of the first Norman custodian of the castle), nearly all the jury, and 100 scholars. Yet strangely the fatal malady affected no women nor anyone who was poor. This inevitably led to rumours of divine influence or sorcery – although the true cause was almost certainly an extreme case of gaol fever (or typhus), a virulent infection spawned by the "nasty and pestilential smell of the prisoners" in the heat of summer. At the time, prisoners were brought to the Shire Hall along a passageway which led directly from their cells, so transmission was quite feasible – although it is again very peculiar that none of the prisoners themselves appear to have perished. Certainly Jencks himself survived, to become a baker in the pro-Catholic environs of Doway (as Wood spelled what was presumably the French town of Douai, near the Belgian border). The tumultuous events of the Black Assize did not save Jencks from his fate, however, and although he lived to an old age – until at least 1610 according to Wood – he did so minus his ears!

Were the lessons of the Black Assize learned? Not according to John Howard, who when visiting the site in 1782 felt it probable that

> the rooms in this castle are the same as the prisoners occupied at the time of the *Black Assize*. The wards, passages and staircases are close and offensive, so that if crowded, I should not greatly wonder to hear of another *fatal assize* at Oxford.

It was an opinion that Edward (alias John) Lambo(u)rn of Nettlebed, John Higden of Wallingford, Mathew Pebworth of Witney, Mathew Smith of Oxford, and David Brod(e)rick of Islip might have shared earlier in the century. All had been sentenced (or "cast", in their parlance) to transportation, and their petition of Michaelmas 1720 advised that they were "in great want and have not sufficient allowance to keep us alive nor nothing to cover our nakedness nor nothing to ley upon butt the bare boards". Rather than endure this situation any longer, their desperation was such that they begged to be "carred to the place which we are cast for or else take us all out and hange us out of such a lingering life". This drastic remedy proved unnecessary. All were transported the following year. But for many others, hanging did indeed mark the termination of their time at Oxford Castle. The following chapter recounts a few of the most remarkable.

CHAPTER FIVE

EXECUTIONS: "THE UNFATHOMABLE GULPH OF ETERNITY"

The preceding chapters concerned a few of the men and women who made a living from their positions of authority within Oxford Castle, and many others whose experience there was not at all of their own free will. The majority of prisoners who escaped found their freedom short-lived. Those transported to the colonies exchanged one form of confinement for another, but, however uncertain and gruelling their prospects, they were at least facing a future with a defined end. Capital convicts too were in no doubt about their fates, once any chance of reprieve had passed – a situation more acceptable to many than months or years of uncertainty. Some seemed positively to welcome what was intended to be a humiliating public death, grasping the opportunity to deliver to the inevitable large crowds which gathered a "gallows speech" of varying degrees of remorse or defiance. And as more and more people found occasion to revel in their last moments, enjoying glory and fame rather than dishonour and shame, the efficacy of public executions began to be questioned – although it took a very long time, until 1863 in fact, for the spectacle ultimately to be abolished.

This final chapter describes a few of Oxford's most remarkable public hangings to the end of Daniel Harris' period as governor of the prison in 1809. The location was always in one of two places: Green Ditch, on the Banbury Road, where the first milestone marked the city boundary, or within the castle precincts. Green Ditch seems to have been where residents of the city were executed, at least until 1757, which is the last occasion specifically identified by *Jackson's Oxford Journal* (see Appendix 2). Much of the information in this chapter comes from *Jackson's*, which seems faithfully to have reported every execution after its launch in 1753. Before that, the sources are less consistent.

Hangings deemed of sufficient interest were often described in broadsheets or longer contemporary pamphlets (held at the Oxfordshire Record Office or Bodleian Library), but the absence of any other records means that a very large number will probably never be revealed. Appendix 1 is, however, as complete a list as has ever previously been compiled. Often the sources do not specify the exact location of the hangings. After 1757 it is likely that they occurred at the castle; from 1787 onwards they certainly did. The main gateway within the newly constructed boundary walls provided an elevated platform from where the gallows could be displayed to maximum effect. The other advantage of this arrangement was that it saw the end of the riotous scenes which had so often accompanied ground-level executions, as the servants of the University's anatomists and the relatives or friends of the deceased fought undignified and often violent battles for possession of the body.

*

FIGURE 16: *The New County Jail with the old Castle Tower, Oxford* as drawn by a pupil of the Oxford artist John Malchair in 1797. The view across New Road shows the main gate, above which executions were held within clear view of the public from 1787. The sturdy walls represent a remarkable transformation of the dilapidated scene of a few years earlier, and one of many building projects of the time in which the governor, Daniel Harris, could take considerable personal pride.
[*Copyright: Bodleian Library, University of Oxford. MS Top. Oxon. c299 f230*]

Oxfordshire murderesses

→>-<+-

Most executions were, unsurprisingly, of men. But the earliest documented case in Oxford concerned a woman: a poor, unexceptional individual in her own right, but one whose fame has outlasted most because of her exceptional ability to cheat the hangman's noose and almost literally rise again from the grave.

"NEWES FROM THE DEAD":
THE RESURRECTION OF ANNE GREEN

Anne Green was hanged at the castle on Saturday 14 December 1650, for the murder of her newborn child. Several contemporary pamphlets, collected at the Bodleian Library under the title *Account of Anne Green* (Bliss B65), tell her story. All agree on the essential details, but the most reliable is *Newes from the Dead*, the author of which was identified by Anthony Wood as Mr Richard Watkins, a sometime student at Christ Church and almost certainly a genuine eye-witness to the events following the hanging. It is this account from which most of the quotations which follow are taken.

Anne Green was a servant at the house of Sir Thomas Read at Duns Tew. Born at Steeple Barton in about 1628, she was described in *Newes from the Dead* as "of a middle stature, strong, fleshie, and of an indifferent good feature". In an age-old scenario, she attracted the unscrupulous attentions of a male member of the household, Mr Jeffrey Read, the 16- or 17-year-old grandson of Sir Thomas, by whom she was "often solicited by fair promises and other amorous enticements".

She managed to hide the inevitable ensuing pregnancy, attending to her duties as normal but with increasing difficulty. One day in November 1650, she was working in Read's malt house when "a child about a span long sprung from her, but abortive, which much improved her health and strength, but being exceedingly fearful that a discovery should be made thereof, she laid it in a corner of the aforesaid house and covered it with dust and rubbish". Another servant discovered her secret, and went straight to inform Sir Thomas. He obliged her to answer immediately to a magistrate, who sent her to Oxford Castle on "an extreme cold and rainy day". There she spent three weeks "in continual affrights and terrors, in a place as comfortless as her condition", awaiting a specially arranged assize court. According to Dr Robert Plot, in *Natural History of Oxfordshire* (1705), the hearing was held in front of Sergeant Umpton Croke of Marston. Despite the likelihood of still-birth, Anne Green was found guilty and sentenced to hang – probably, one suspects, to satisfy the Reads' desire that suspicions about the behaviour of certain of their family might be laid to rest with her. It was not to be.

At the execution, Green exhibited "an undauntedness of spirit" and "at the going up the ladder, she fixt her eyes on the executioner, saying, God forgive my false accusers, as I freely forgive thee". In a short address to the crowd, she said that her impending death "doth not in the least strike dread and terror to my heart, but rather incites me to a notion of eternal joy and happiness, for I conceive there is no more than this rope and ladder between me and Heaven". She remained hanging for half an hour. This was more than a century before the introduction of the "drop" (first used at Tyburn in 1759 and universally in 1783), when death would be instantaneous as the victim's neck was broken as a result of the sudden fall. Before then, hanging meant slow asphyxiation, and it was common practice to ask friends and relatives (a cousin, in Green's case) to try to speed the process up. *Newes from the Dead* described the scene:

> some of her friends in the meantime thumping her on the breast, others hanging with all their weight upon her legges, sometimes lifting her up, and then pulling her downe again with a suddaine jerke, thereby the sooner to dispatch her out of her paine: insomuch as the under-sheriffe fearing lest thereby they should break the rope, forbad them to do so any longer.

In addition: "A soldier standing by gave her 4 or 5 blowes on the brest, with the but end of his musket." Having thus established that the young woman had truly expired, her body was taken to the house of Mr Clark, an apothecary, for dissection. Before any medical men had arrived, however, some lingering signs of life were detected, so "a lusty fellow that stood by (thinking to do an act of charity in ridding her out of the small reliques of a painful life) stamped several times on her breast and stomach with all the force he could". Plot named this man as Mason, a taylor, and added that further blows were struck with the butt end of a musket by a soldier, whom he identified as Orum. Yet despite all, Anne Green refused to die. A Dr William Petty of Brasenose College arrived at about 9am, and, still

FIGURE 17: The woodcut accompanying *Newes from the dead* (1651), showing the crime and execution of Anne Green. Note the man pulling down on her legs and the soldier striking her with his musket.
[*Copyright: Bodleian Library, University of Oxford. Bliss B65, p.1.*]

detecting signs of life, attempted various treatments to revive her. This included the standard measure of bleeding. Still insensible, she was left to sleep, a woman being brought in to lie next to her to keep her warm through the night.

The next day, Sunday, Petty and some other doctors returned at 8am, to find her recovered and talking, though obviously still in pain, and around 9am "she laughed and talked merrily, looking fresh and of a good colour". On Monday the doctors questioned her in private about her recollections. She answered "that after she put off some of her clothes, bequeathing them to her mother (which was early in the morning, before her execution) and heard someone say that one of the prisoners was let out of the chaine to put her to death, she remembered nothing at all". This was not the exclusive glimpse of the afterlife that the Oxford academics had been hoping for, but despite all entreaties, Anne Green was never able to recollect what had happened after her fetters had been removed, save for a vague recollection of "a fellow wrapt up in a blanket, which indeed was the habit of the executioner". *Newes from the Dead* attributed this to "her spirits at that time being either so fixed or benummed with feare, as not to admit of any new impressions, or otherwise so turbulent and unquiet as presently to discompose and obliterate them".

As news spread of this minor miracle, an armed guard was needed to keep away the inquisitive crowds. Anne's father was no fool, and realised that his daughter had changed overnight from a cause of disgrace for the family to one of great value. Consequently he stationed himself at the house, in order to accept donations from "those of the better sort" who wished to get a glimpse of his daughter. These funds paid for the apothecary's bill, her food and lodging, and part of the cost of her eventual pardon. By the 19th, five days after the hanging, she had recovered sufficiently to walk with assistance, and to eat her first substantial food, and eight to ten days later she went to stay with friends in her home village of Steeple Barton, "taking away with her the coffin wherein she lay as a trophy of this her wonderful preservation". There she married, said Plot, and bore three children.

An event of this magnitude brought the ballad writers out in force. One short poem from Edward Norreys Esq. is notable for being addressed not to Anne but to her would-be executioner:

> To the hangman:
> Come *Flesh-Crow*, tell me, what's the Cause that you
> Rigour to Men, to Women favour show?
> Your Office you have not performed, 'tis plaine:
> See, here's the Wench you hanged, alive againe.
> Yet for this once, I'le cleare you, it was not
> Your *slack rope* saved her, nor your *fast-loose* knot.
> Her fatall halter thee (to end the strife)
> Untwisted spun into a thread of life.

Anne Green's "thread of life" came to an end in 1659, according to Plot. It is hugely poignant that the life of her persecutor, Sir Thomas Read, in contrast, ended only a few days after her recovery. His burial at Duns Tew on 20 December occurred just as his former servant was starting to walk and eat again. Many no doubt saw this as a sign from God. Anne Green's "resurrection" was certainly seen as such, and she was pardoned of her supposed crime. The story of another woman whose circumstances eight years later were very similar had a much less happy ending, however.

A POOR MAID FROM MAGDALEN PARISH

Anthony Wood is the original source for the story of a second botched execution. He recorded in *Life and Times* the hanging at Green Ditch on Tuesday 4 May 1658 of a maid for murdering her newborn illegitimate child. Plot later identified her as Elizabeth, the servant of Mrs Cope of Magdalen parish, and claimed that she

> hung for so long that one of the by-standers scrupled not to say that if she were not dead he would be hanged for her: hereupon being cut down (the gallows being very high) she fell with such violence on the ground that it would have been enough to have been the death of many another person, only to have had such a fall.

Her body was taken away to be dissected, but, like the resilient Anne Green, she was found to be still alive, and taken to The George Inn in Magdalen parish (according to Plot), where a St John's College physician, Dr William Coniers, was able to attend to her. Also like Green, she underwent bleeding and had another woman sleep next to her for warmth.

So far so good. But when the city bailiffs heard what had happened, they went to where Elizabeth was recovering soon after midnight, intent on finishing the job. She was conveyed to Broken Hayes (now Gloucester Green, but extending also south of George Street – see FIGURE 8), where the bailiffs "put a halter about her neck and plucked her out of a coffin over one of the trees there". This time there was no mistake, but local people were so enraged by this behaviour that the tree in question was felled in protest. Henry Mallory, the bailiff most responsible, was vilified thereafter, and he had to cease trading as a cutler, the general opinion being that his subsequent impoverishment was because "God's judgements followed him for the cruelty he shew'd to the poore maid".

INFANTICIDE — AN EXCLUSIVELY FEMALE CRIME

Several other young women were executed in Oxford for this same offence of infanticide over the next century. One named by Wood was Alice Carpenter of Botley, who was hanged at Green Ditch on 4 May 1680. She was a servant to a smith called Brummigam in St Peter-in-the-East. Another case (possibly fictional) is commemorated in a 1716 ballad entitled *The Oxford Tragedy or The Sorrowful Lamentation of Sarah Sparrow, who is condemn'd for the murther of her bastard child.* The father was her own brother, and both lived in Oxford.*

There were doubtless many more such cases, the records of which have not survived, and it again takes the introduction of *Jackson's Oxford Journal* to furnish more complete details. Two more executions of infanticides are

---

* The name 'Sarah' in the copy of this printed ballad held at the Bodliean Library (fol. THETA 662/7) has been amended in ink with Jane in the title and Anna elsewhere.

covered in its pages. One was on 31 July 1762, when Susan Harris, a servant to a farmer called Mr Taylor of Sydenham, met her end (simultaneously with James Costard of Benson, who had been found guilty of the murder of his mother, who expired instantly when he fired a pistol "so close to her as to set her cap and handkerchief on fire"). Harris had delivered herself of a baby girl at around 3am one morning, and when Taylor's wife, who had long suspected her of being pregnant, went up to her room at 5am "the child was found in a cupboard in her bed-chamber wrapped up in a sheet". Both Costard and Harris behaved "very decently" at their execution. *Jackson's* quoted Harris' last words as: "Father pray for me, Mother pray for me, good people, all pray for me". Then came a clue as to how Anne Green and the maid known only as Elizabeth might have survived their ordeals: "Before the cart drew away, she sank down and thereby the knot slipping to her chin, the noose did not draw, and they were obliged to raise a ladder, and lift up the body, till the cord was better fixed."

The final incident, and indeed the last hanging of any woman in Oxford, occurred on 10 March 1766. But it was an incident with a twist, because it was not the mother of the newborn child who was found guilty of murdering it, but the grandmother. Mary Lampry[*] and her daughter Ann had been at work in the fields near their Kingham home the previous August. When the sound of an infant's cries attracted the attention of some other labourers, the two women attempted to behave as if nothing was wrong, but the tiny body was found "dead upon the ground under one of them, wrapped up in a piece of flannel". The conclusion was that "it had not only been strangled with a cord but that its body was also crushed flat by having been set or laid upon". Mary Lampry was sent immediately to the castle; Ann followed a month later, when she had recovered her strength. Both were condemned to death at the following March Assizes, but only Mary suffered that fate, confessing only a few minutes before her execution that "she was the sole cause of the child's death, and that her

---

[*] William Lampry married Mary Greyhurst of Kingham at Chipping Norton on 30 January 1732. Their daughter Ann was baptised at Kingham on 5 June 1738. William was buried in 1755; to compound the tragedy of the Lampry family, he had hanged himself.

daughter was perfectly innocent, and in a swoon during the whole of that transaction". Ann was consequently granted an initial respite of ten days, and ultimately given a free pardon.

"GENTLEMEN, DO NOT HANG ME HIGH":
MARY BLANDY OF HENLEY

There was no such reprieve for Mary Blandy, the most famous eighteenth-century woman to be executed at Oxford Castle, though she continued to hope for clemency right to the end. Blandy was an exception to the general rule of a person from an impoverished background turning to crime as a means of improving a miserable and downtrodden existence. For she was the daughter of an eminent attorney, Francis Blandy, who was also Henley's Town Clerk – and it was her own father who was the victim. In a way he was the author of his own misfortune. Mary, an only child, was in her thirties and showing no likelihood of finding a husband.* When his wife died in October 1749, Francis contrived to improve Mary's chances by exaggerating the extent of his wealth, and therefore of Mary's inheritance.

The ploy worked – but not entirely satisfactorily. A Scottish army captain called William Cranston became suddenly enamoured of Mary, and she of him. A Scottish army captain, however, was not the sort of match that Francis had had in mind, so he obstructed the romance, and banned Cranston from seeing her. The two lovers concluded that Francis was an obstacle which had to be removed. Back in Scotland (where it later transpired that he already had a wife in any case), Cranston contrived a plan whereby he would send Mary some arsenic powder, and she would administer it in his food. Sadly for Cranston, Mary proved an incompetent would-be patricide; before her father finally succumbed on 14 August 1751, the family's washerwoman, chambermaid, and cat had

---

* Quite why this should be is not clear. Even in one of the many contemporary publications which were hostile to her case she was described as "of middle size, well-shaped, of a brown complexion, with black eyes, full of fire, and tho' not a beauty, is very agreeable, especially when she speaks, and her conversation is full of wit and good sense".

FIGURE 18: An image from *A Genuine Account* ..., one of many contemporary
publications relating to Mary Blandy, showing her taking tea with a friend,
to all appearances as if she were entertaining at her home in Henley.
Only the small fetters around her ankles show that all is not as it seems.
[*Copyright: Oxfordshire County Record Office*]

all nearly died as a result of consuming the tainted remains of Francis' unfinished food!

Despite all the evidence, the Henley authorities were reluctant to accept that a likeable young woman from their own social elite could commit such a deed. The townspeople were less sceptical, however, and when Mary attempted to leave with indecent haste they took it upon themselves to prevent her. As a result, she got no further than The Angel Inn, on the Berkshire side of the Thames, while the mob lurked outside. It was a situation which gave the still slightly apologetic Henley authorities the pretext they needed – to arrest her for her own safety. When the autopsy revealed considerable quantities of arsenic in the dead man's stomach, though, an inevitable conclusion was drawn, and she was taken to Oxford Castle early on 16 August, having been obliged to remain inside her house and therefore to miss Francis' funeral the previous day.

For some reason – probably while a fruitless search was undertaken to trace the devious Cranston – her trial was delayed for more than six months. Her stay in the castle was by no means as unpleasant as for many. A woman of her standing was permitted her own room in the prison (seemingly within the house provided for the gaoler William Wisdom himself), to have a maid in attendance, and to entertain visitors. As an account published prior to the trial stated, she was "serene and calm … always drinking tea twice a day, sometimes walking in the keepers garden with a guard, and playing at cards in the evening".

Numerous other pamphlets were published before and after her trial (in February 1752) and execution. One (*Miss Mary Blandy's own Account*, printed by William Jackson himself, from where most of the quotations below derive) reported a false rumour about the day of her execution resulted in numerous people gathering at the Castle Green. Blandy

> went up several times into the rooms facing the Green, where she could view the great crowd of people about it, which she did with all the calmness and unconcern imaginable, and only said she would not balk their expectations, tho' her execution might be deferred a day or two longer.

It was, until the following Monday, April 6th. At 10pm on the Sunday, hearing that the sheriff was in town, a necessary precursor to any execution, Blandy requested that she should not be disturbed before 8am. During the night she arose at 4am and went to the upper rooms of the house to look upon the gallows, which were "opposite the door of the gaol, and made by laying a poll [sic] across upon the arms of two trees". At 8.30 she spent 30 minutes in prayer with the prison chaplain, the Reverend Mr Swinton, who failed to persuade her to acknowledge her guilt. She was then led to the gallows, holding two guineas in her hand for the executioner.*

Blandy was a member of the establishment, for whom appearances counted – even at the very last moment. Her attire was therefore carefully chosen, and equally carefully described in all the accounts, as a black Bombazine short sack (a loose-fitting gown) and petticoat, with a clean white handkerchief drawn over her face. Her hands were tied with a strong black ribbon – a Paduasoy ribbon, in fact, as one writer found it necessary to specify!

Before ascending the ladder, Blandy made the expected and customary speech, and, still maintaining her innocence, "behaved with such serenity and composure, and with such a decent resolution, as greatly surprised and charmed many of the spectators". Depending which account you choose to believe, those spectators numbered either 5,000 or very few. Either way, "contrary to what is observed at other executions, there was almost profound silence" as many of those present were moved to tears.

On the fifth step of the ladder, she uttered the words which had a partic-ular significance for any female, conscious of the likely presence in the crowd of men seeking a cheap thrill: "Gentlemen, do not hang me high for the sake of decency", she requested, before ascending two more steps. Then the halter was put about her neck, and the ladder was turned. In accor-dance with her request, her feet almost touched the ground, so her modesty was preserved – at least for the half-hour her body remained suspended.

---

* The word "tree" was often employed to mean "gallows" and implies the upright posts or gibbet, not a living tree. It was common practice for the condemned person, from royalty downwards, to provide remuneration to the executioner, purportedly to encourage a swift and efficient job.

But no-one seemed to have thought to provide a coffin. Perhaps the confusion about the day of execution had deterred those who might otherwise have made the journey from Henley; perhaps there was an expectation that an otherwise blameless woman of her rank would, in the end, somehow manage to acquire a reprieve. Whatever, with no coffin available, her body "was carried through the crowd upon the shoulders of one of the sheriff's men in the most beastly manner, with her legs exposed very indecently for several hundred yards, and then deposited in the sheriff's man's house". A hearse was found and departed at 5.30pm for Henley, where Mary Blandy was interred the same night in the chancel of the church, next to both her mother and the father of whose death she had been the cause.*

Mary Blandy's incompetent and blatant murder of her father was a rare exception to the crimes for which almost all other women were executed in Oxford, namely the murder of their own illegitimate children. Very few suffered for any other reason. A thief called Margaret Dunn was one in 1754, and in 1723 Joanna Mead of Combe had been executed for poisoning her husband – the specific penalty for that being death by burning, the only such occurrence noted (by Thomas Hearne, the Oxford diarist). The executions of only eleven women, at both Green Ditch and Oxford Castle, can be discerned between 1650 and 1766 (see Appendix 1). Only two were for murder other than infanticide.

---

* The register of St Mary's, Henley, records Francis Blandy's burial on 17 August 1751, with the added comment: "Attorney at Law was poysoned by his only child Mary Blandy". Mary Blandy's entry for 6 April 1752 has also been annotated to the effect that she had "poysoned" her father. Cranston had fled the country in February, and died of natural causes in Flanders before the end of the year.

*

Oxfordshire murderers

➤➤━◄━

One might expect that the scarcity of murderesses in the Oxford annals would be counterbalanced by a very much larger number of men. Surprisingly perhaps, that is not the case. The most intriguing case in the eighteenth century (featured in *The Abingdon Waterturnpike Murder*) concerned the death of an elderly pedlar as he walked home alongside the River Thames one evening in October 1787. Three men were executed for the crime: John Castle and Charles Evans Shury on 19 July 1790, and Giles Freeman Covington on 7 March 1791. In terms of murder for personal gain, this appears to have been the only instance in Oxfordshire – or at least the only one that the authorities brought to any conclusion. All the other murders by men – and there seem to have been only 13 punished by death in Oxford between 1650 and 1800 – concerned victims with whom they were already intimate.

"AS INNOCENT ... AS THE CHILD THAT IS UNBORN": JOHN PROTHEROE OF OXFORD

One of these victims was the pregnant wife of John Protheroe, who was executed for her murder on Monday 22 March 1725. Never named, she had taken to spending more and more time with the owners and customers of the ale-house next door to their home in Barton. As a consequence, Protheroe found "his wife's love in a declining condition towards him and his family", and in retaliation took her life one night, through the use of physical force. At least that is what the jury found. A broadsheet published at the time presented the situation in such a way that the 33-year-old Protheroe appeared, on the contrary, "as innocent ... as the child that is unborn". Thomas Hearne's comments in respect of this particular broadsheet reflect the caution needed in assessing the veracity of all such publications. The copy at the Bodleian Library (MS Hearne's Diary 107) is annotated in Hearne's own hand, in which he identifies Mary Bailey and Sampson Bowles as the people who, over a period of 18 months, were supposed to have "oftentimes by perswasion and once by force attempted to debauch" Protheroe's wife. Hearne denounced this and the rest of the broadsheet as a "downright formal lye", saying that Protheroe "had been a sad, vile wretch and is said to have murdered one of his children before. Not one person appeared in his behalf, no not even at his execution, even so much as to take care of his corps".

A "DIABOLICAL INSTANCE OF BARBARITY": ROBERT HITCHCOCK OF COMBE

Of the other men executed at Oxford for murder in the eighteenth century, three are of particular interest. On Monday 9 March 1777, Robert Hitchcock, a wealthy farmer from Combe, near Woodstock, was executed for what a broadsheet described uncompromisingly as "the most diabolical instance of barbarity ever remembered in a civilised nation". This was the murder of his 81-year-old father, Edward, in the previous July. Hitchcock had hardly been subtle about his "barbarity". In *Jackson's* account of the trial, 13 witnesses swore that "in the course of a few hours they saw the prisoner beat, bruise, and kick his aged parent upon the road in his way from Bloxham to Combe in a most shocking and inhuman manner". The two men took until 3am to complete their 14-mile journey, and Edward was found dead the following morning.

During the four-hour trial, Hitchcock, who was aged about 40, remained unrepentant, even though his only defence was that his father was "frequently insane and subject to fits". The broadsheet, with a point to make to substantiate its sensational claim, advised that the son was known to have "long forced him to undergo labour beyond his strength, and after cruelly beating and whipping the old man, whilst fainting under the fatigue, frequently to have tied him to the harness of his horses and let the team drag him along".

On the day of the execution, Hitchcock showed greater penitence.

Poignantly dressed in the same clothes that he had worn at his father's funeral, he spent 15 minutes in prayer beneath the gallows, and specifically requested that his body might be delivered to the surgeons "without molestation". He need not have worried: the undignified scenes of riot which marked the conclusion of so many executions did not occur, as there were no sympathisers ready to try to claim the body before the agents of the Christ Church Anatomy School – certainly not his wife, one suspects, from the fact that she remarried the very next month, considerably the richer for having inherited Hitchcock's sizeable fortune.

"CUT OFF FROM THE FACE OF THE EARTH":
GEORGE STRAP OF BICESTER

An exception to the murder of a relative concerned George Strap, who was executed on Monday 13 March 1775 for killing his master, Edward Bowden of Bicester. When Bowden, a cobbler, failed to open his shop one morning, the alarm was raised. Strap gallantly offered to ascend a ladder in order to look inside, but "it was observed that before he was high enough to see into the room, he told the people assembled that his master had not been in bed". Mistake number one. Deciding to break in to ascertain the truth, the gathered neighbours found Bowden's body inside. He had been hit on the head with a hammer, and his throat had been slit. With suspicions already aroused, Strap made his second mistake, by allowing himself to be surprised a little later in the act of trying to wash blood from his clothes – a man caught literally red-handed, then, in the accepted origin of the phrase. The motive was afterwards assumed to have been greed: Bowden was known to have told Strap that he had 15 guineas on him. At the trial, Strap persisted in his innocence at first, but ultimately acknowledged his guilt. The long eloquent verdict delivered by Justice Nares concluded with the phrase that "you are to be cut off from the face of the earth", to which, according to a broadsheet, Strap responded, "I say so too."

DEATH OF A BARMAID:
EDWARD THORN OF HENLEY

The final case of murder within the period covered by this book concerned probably the oldest person executed at Oxford, Edward Thorn. Thorn was baptised at Steventon on 30 November 1740, and died on Monday 28 July 1800.* The previous March, Amy Jacob, a servant at The White Hart at Northfield End, Henley, of which Thorn was the landlord, was discovered dead. The inquest showed she had been poisoned, but revealed too another pertinent fact – that she was pregnant. Suspicions were aroused when Thorn absconded before the coroner had reached a decision, and his case was hardly helped by the evidence of a Henley apothecary, who testified that Thorn had earlier asked for advice on how to terminate a pregnancy. A few days later, Thorn had purchased some ratsbane, the same poison as was discovered in the girl's stomach. At the trial, the judge underlined that even if "the fatal drug was administered to cause abortion, it was equally criminal in the eye of the law as if given to destroy the life of the girl". We have read of several young women condemned for their futile attempts to cover up an illegitimate birth. Thorn had ensured that Amy Jacob was required to face no such choice.

In the cases of murder outlined above, the intimacy between the perpetrator and victim is a common factor. Occasionally, however, members of the same family were *united* in committing a crime deemed worthy of capital punishment. The previous chapter revealed the cases of the Druets (Drewetts), Colletts, Gullivers, and Crook(e)s, all of whose sentences were reprieved to transportation. Two sets of brothers, however, suffered the ultimate penalty at Oxford, for crimes of rather less gravity than murder...

---

* Thorn could have been outlived by Shadrack Smith, a Gypsy described by *Jackson's* as "near 60 years of age" when executed on 22 March 1762. Smith was born in Norwood, Essex, but on what date is not known. His crime had been to threaten and rob a young woman in the Charlbury area, and he was convicted on the evidence of his own son, leading him to caution all parents "not to put their lives into the hands of their children".

Of highwaymen and horse-thieves

→>-<←

THE BROTHERS WILLIAMS AND COX

On Monday 28 August 1766, John Williams of Beckley in Northampton-shire and John Milward (alias Brown) from the same county were hanged at Oxford for highway robbery. The previous March they had deprived Mrs Rachel Newell of Stokenchurch of nearly ten guineas as she travelled between her home and West Wycombe (in Buckinghamshire) one evening. Both young men, they had known each other only a matter of days, and claimed that this was the only crime of any consequence they had committed. Often youth was seen as an extenuating circum-stance, deserving of the reprieve of transportation. Milward and Williams were not so fortunate. At their execution, Milward met every expectation of the crowd in providing a spirited speech from the gallows. *Jackson's* reported that he "harangued the populace for some time", saying that "Sabbath-breaking and bad company had brought upon them their present misfortune", and "begging that their dreadful example might be a warning to others". Indeed, with admirable aplomb, he delivered a warning of his own, "that the age was indeed arrived at so high a pitch of wickedness … that it was not uncommon for people who live by thieving to attend executions in order to pick pockets". No doubt gaining many new admirers with his performance, Milward "met his fate with great courage, shaking hands with many people near the cart, and desiring the prayers of the spectators". Williams was much less forthcoming, but his brother, James, who followed him to the gallows all of 24 years later, had more to say – albeit, under the circumstances, what he actually said was of truly touching naivety.

James Williams was one four men whose association with the habitual horse-thief, Thomas "Oxford Tom" Smith (alias Davis), had fatal consequences. Smith's confession prior to his own execution at Oxford in March 1790 occasioned the subsequent arrest and executions of the Abingdon Waterturnpike murderers: John Castle, Charles Evans Shury, and Giles Freeman Covington. James Williams was more directly associated with Smith than these three men. Described by *Jackson's* as "rather more ignorant in many respects than is even common to labouring men", he had moved from his native Beckley to find employment with different farmers near Wheatley, Thame, and Bletchingdon. He then went to London, having seemingly driven his employer's sheep to Smithfield to sell, pocketed the money, and never returned. He made the acquaintance of Smith at Moorfields, and within five weeks the two men contrived to steal a mare, saddle, and colt from Williams' former master, Thomas Juggins of Wheatley, early in 1790. Their subsequent arrest was due, not so much to the efforts of the hard-pressed forces of law and order, but to Juggins' own determination to regain his property. *Jackson's* of 3 April 1790 praised him (and another victim of Smith's predilection for other people's horses, Simon Peck of Rye Farm near Abingdon) for his "laudable spirit, almost regardless of either fatigue or expense" in bringing Williams and "Oxford Tom" to justice. At the execution on Monday 2 August 1790, still protesting innocence, Williams seemed quite unaffected, according to a broadsheet recording the event, his last words being merely " 'My boys, take warning, for I am just going! But my cap will blow off, won't it?', and in that hardened state of insensitivity the poor wretch was launched into eternity", the loss of his headgear being the least of his worries, one would have thought!

Whereas a gap of more than two decades separated the executions of the two Williams brothers, the other siblings executed at Oxford, John and Richard Cox, met their ends together, in literally touching circumstances. They were not alone on the scaffold on Monday 27 March 1786. With them were Miles Ward and John Grace, executed for two different crimes, making this the largest number of people simultaneously executed at Oxford. John (31) and Richard (21) Cox were members of what *Jackson's* called "a gang of villains who have long infested Henley and its neighbourhood". They were found guilty of stealing lead and sheep through the revelations of John Perrin, an accomplice, who, unwisely and unusually, "kept a regular journal of their transactions for a series of years".

John Grace (24) was also found guilty of stealing sheep; Miles Ward (21) of theft of silverware from the chapel of Magdalen College. At the execution,

> Ward behaved himself in a manner very suitable to his situation; he prayed fervently and shed tears abundantly, yet with a becoming firmness; Grace and the elder Cox shewed also a proper sense of the near approach of death, but the younger of the Coxes seemed either hardened or stupefied in his last moments. When all four, standing up in the cart, were tied up to the gallows, Ward, with great composure, asked his companions *Are you all ready to die? If you are, let us take leave of one another.* They then all shook hands, and the cart drawing away before the brothers had quitted each other's hold, they long remained with the hands of each strongly clasped together.

"PLUNDERINGS AND DEVASTATIONS":
WILLIAM HYDE OF STANTON ST JOHN

Another man who had "behaved himself in a manner very suitable to his situation" when facing the gallows in Oxford a few years earlier was William Hyde, one of Oxfordshire's most colourful criminals of the period. Hyde is a classic example of a talented man who squandered all for the lack of a little willpower. Born in Stanton St John, Hyde was a bright child and had soon mastered his father's trade of sieve-making, "in which employment ...", according to a broadsheet of his life, "... he was equalled by few and excelled by none; nay so excellent were his talents that there are very few handycraft trades in which he did not exhibit wonderful abilities". He was also "an excellent tinker, basket maker and chair maker, a good cobbler, and one of the very best hands in the husbandry business this day in *England.*" Furthermore "in the employment of hedging, ditching and planting of beans, or hoeing of turnips, he would alone do as much as any two men in the country."

One might suspect a degree of bias in such a fulsome appraisal, akin to the propagandist intentions of the earlier broadsheet of John Protheroe, perhaps, but the writer continues to suggest that all this industry was merely "a cover for his rogueries". These included two instances of "unlawfully lopping, and otherwise damaging certain timber trees in the woods" belonging to St John's College near Stanton St John, for which he spent a total of 18 months inside Oxford Castle. In fact, not quite the full 18 months, since he accepted the alternative of enlisting in the marines early in 1777, but then took the drastic measure of cutting off his own right thumb to obtain a discharge after three months in the service.

Immediately on his release in May 1777, Hyde abandoned his wife and four children* for a petty thief called Mary Makemalt. It was with her that he committed the crime that would earn him the death penalty, namely burgling the house of Richard Banes (or Bean) of Old Cutteslowe on 19 October. It was a crime where alcohol played its part in a wanton display of cheek, as the two thieves "regaled themselves not only with eggs and bacon, but had also beat up some batter, fried pancakes, and supplied themselves plentifully from the cellar".

It might have been one of the last good meals Hyde enjoyed! Both he and Makemalt were apprehended and taken to the castle to await the assizes in March. He received the death penalty, and there are hints of a tangled love-life in the fact that (surely in the spirit of a jilted lover?) the principal evidence against the pair was one Mary Allen, described as another of Hyde's "pillow companions".

On the Saturday before the execution Hyde was visited by his mother and neighbours from Stanton. These, presumably, were not the same neighbours as those who apparently "dreaded his appearance near their

---

* His wife's name was Hannah, and their children were Mary, baptised at Stanton St John in 1767, Elizabeth in 1769, Patience in 1773, and Phoebe in 1775. Hyde, spelled Hide, is presumably the same as was baptised by William and Martha Hide on 21 July 1746 – even though the broadsheet gave his year of birth as 1749.

habitations, for his departure was generally attended by a discovery of plunderings and devastations". Friends came too, and when it was suggested to Hyde that rather than have so many visitors "his mind might be more collected and his time better spent by withdrawing to the chapel, he replied with great composure that the chapel was a very cold place". He retained his dignified calm to the end, which was on Monday 22 March 1779, his undoubted talent wasted simply for a self-confessed weakness for "Sabbath-breaking, loose company and drunkenness".

There are many other examples of thefts, particularly of livestock, attracting capital punishment at Oxford Castle in the eighteenth century, and a comparable number for highway robbery. This was a crime which grew through the century to be imbued with a romance which, if the highwayman exhibited sufficient civility to his victims, accorded the perpetrators a degree of admiration unknown to the petty thief or fraudster. Head and shoulders above all those executed in Oxford was the highwayman Isaac Darkin (alias Dumas).

"JOY TO THEE, LOVELY THIEF!": ISAAC DARKING (ALIAS DUMAS)

Although Darkin was only about 21 when he died, his fame was such that several versions of his life were published within days of his death, on Monday 23 March 1761. Many were spurious, and the details that follow are taken from *Jackson's* and (in respect of his early life) a pamphlet printed specifically for William Jackson (and endorsed by William Wisdom, the gaoler) entitled *The Authentic Trial and Memoirs of Isaac Darkin alias Dumas*.

Darkin was born the son of a cork-cutter in London's Eastcheap district, in about 1740. When his father died in about 1754, Darkin and his step-sister took over the business, but decided to close it four years later. It was at this point that Darkin was drawn to a life of crime, in order to support a lifestyle of great extravagance and many mistresses. He enjoyed nine months of success in the Essex area, but was eventually apprehended for a highway robbery, and given a capital sentence at his trial in Chelmsford in February 1758. At the following assizes, he was reprieved on account of his youth and later pardoned on the condition that he serve in the forces in Antigua. His vessel sailed in January 1759. In Antigua, Darkin proved "much superior in capacity to the people who are generally met with in the station", and though he struggled with the discipline (being court-martialled three times in the seven weeks that he remained in service), he was sufficiently personable to be appointed to the relatively undemanding role of servant to an officer.

However, Darkin yearned for home, and somehow persuaded the captain of a merchant ship to smuggle him back to England, even though this offence carried a penalty of £100. He was back on English soil about nine months after leaving, and soon resumed his old ways. Finding himself suspected, however, he took a route chosen by many men on the run – the Navy. Darkin was no ordinary fugitive, however. He found that the Navy gave him not a new direction in life, but excellent cover to enable him to continue his old one, as he contrived to commit robberies while on furloughs from his ship. He was accused of the robbery on 22 June 1760 of Lord Percival, and was held at Salisbury. Found not guilty, he committed another robbery six weeks after his release. It would be his last. His fame was now too great for there to be any doubt that it was he who deprived a Smithfield apothecary, Robert Gammon, of a gold watch, one guinea, and five shillings on the highway near Nettlebed. He was arrested by some of the unofficial network of "thief-takers" employed by Sir John Fielding in London, and taken to Newgate, before being transferred to Oxford Castle in January 1761 to stand trial at the following assizes.

Jackson's was especially adoring when reporting his imminent arrival from Newgate, describing him as "a lively and facetious companion, and is said to sing an excellent song, on which account we hope the governor will accommodate him with an elegant apartment, for the more commodious exhibition of his agreeable talents". The next week, *Jackson's* reported visits "by many gentlemen of the University of all ranks and degrees", and with touching concern, added that many of them "in consideration of his proper deportment under his present unhappy circumstances, have generously contributed to relieve the expenses and anxieties of a tedious confinement". Evidently, a rumour spread that among these contributions were a University gown and cap to try to help him escape, because William Wisdom was later obliged to deny this in a notice of 18 April 1761.

At his trial in March, Darkin's defence was weak, based essentially on having not prepared one! Evidently lulled by his popularity (particularly with the opposite sex and members of the University), he had assumed that he would be pardoned again. This time there was no reprieve, however. During his final days at the castle, he read the *Beggar's Opera*, according to *Jackson's*, and "appeared to enter thoroughly into the spirit of *Mackheath's part*, and seemed greatly to enjoy the character".* Dashing to the last, he had "a taste for elegance in every respect, was remarkably fond of silk stockings, and neat in his linnen, had his hair dressed in the most fashionable manner every morning, his polished fetters were supported round his waist by a sword belt, and tied up at the knees with ribbon".

Darkin's wardrobe on the day of the execution was also described: a mourning suit comprising a striped waistcoat under a black one, with a clean ruffled shirt. After he had received the sacrament, "one of the prisoners that was to be hangman was called in and his arms were tied behind his back with a black ribbon". Darkin knelt and prayed at the foot of the ladder, ascended it quickly, then

> pulled off his neckcloth, unbuttoned the collar of his shirt and waistcoat, and put the rope about his neck. Then pulling a white handkerchief out of his pocket, which he tied over his face, and several times asking the populace to hang upon him, he turned his back to the ladder, and himself fixing the rope, in a moment dropped his neckcloth as a signal, but without waiting for the ladder's being turned, stepped off.

* John Gay's musical play opened in January 1728, and was easily the biggest musical hit of the eighteenth century. It tells of the relationship between a highwayman, Captain Macheath, and the daughter of a thief-taker, Polly Peachum.

Another, generally sensationalised, account entitled *The Genuine Life of Isaac Darking alias Dumas* corroborated this, saying that "after the fatal cord was fastened, he turned himself off, with some eagerness, to explore the unfathomable gulph of eternity".

Newspapers were often generous in their praise of those facing execution with penitence and dignity. In Darkin's case, *Jackson's* verged on hero worship, saying "his behaviour in his last moments was entirely correspondent to the steadiness of character and intrepidity which he affected and maintained even in his most dangerous enterprises". The body remained hanging for nearly an hour, and was then taken to St Thomas' Church by bargemen, "in triumph", according to *Jackson's*, and "most inhumanly mangled, in order to prevent (according to his request) his being anatomised". The author of *The Genuine Life* provided more precise details, saying that he had left the bargemen five guineas "to save him from the hands of surgeons who waited for his body in order to dissect it. But to render their design abortive, the bargemen cut open his body, took out his bowels, and filled it with lime." This gruesome news caused *Jackson's* to muse that "could he have foreseen this treatment, he would perhaps have shewn less reluctance". William Jackson's authorised *Authentic Trial and Memoirs* added a further ghoulish detail, that the bargemen then "opened the grave where Grindey was buried, who was hanged some years ago for returning from transportation, and buried him in that coffin".*

It was a gruesome end for a young man who had captured the public imagination with his daring exploits, his decent behaviour, and beguiling charm. Many a female tear was probably shed at the time. Prior to his death he had expressed the hope that "he should not see any women among the spectators, as that would affect him greatly, for they had been his ruin". He wasn't the first or last condemned man to express such sentiments, but for Darkin the association was undeniable. During

---

* William Grindy was committed to Oxford Castle on 5 August 1752 "for returning from trans-portation before time expired". He was missing by Easter 1753, but there is no record of either his burial or Darkin's at St Thomas' Church.

his confinement at Salisbury, the writer of *The Authentic Trial and Memoirs* claimed that

> his sufferings made a deep impression upon the tender hearts of the ladies, some of whom having visited him in his confinement, his obliging manner, genteel address, lively disposition, and whole deportment, so struck them that his fame soon became the discourse of the tea table.

One consequence was this verse, the first of five composed by "certain belles who visited him in prison":

> Joy to thee, lovely thief! That thou
> Hast 'scap'd the fatal string.
> Let gallows groan with ugly rogues
> Dumas must never swing.

The author made no comment on the quality of the verse, but, with advantage of hindsight, observed only that the ladies were "not good at prognostication"!

The extreme precautions taken by Darkin to thwart the agents of the University's anatomists are indicative of the horror with which this "deterrent" was viewed in the public mind when it was instigated by law as the ultimate fate of the bodies of executed criminals in 1751. In fact, the law was intended to apply to murderers only, but such was the demand for bodies (and the lack of Oxfordshire murderers) that the corpse of almost anyone became fair game.*

---

* A prime example of this was at the execution at the castle of a sheep-thief called Robert Randall in May 1755. During the execution a dispute arose over rights to the body, which "occasioned a pitch'd battle" between a "celebrated champion" called James Carter and a bargeman called William Briscoe. They settled their differences at the Holywell Cockpit the same afternoon, when "Carter shewed himself thoroughly *game* by giving out thoroughly satisfied in about three minutes." (*Jackson's* 3 May 1755)

The "reformed mode" of execution

-+->-<+-

The public were rarely prevented from gathering close to the gallows, and the requests made by Darkin and Anne Green, for people to pull down on their legs to hasten the moment of death, would have found many takers. It was in any case considered by many to be efficacious to touch the corpse of an executed person, or to purchase their clothing or a piece of the rope (an additional accepted reward for the hangman). Disorder was therefore almost inevitable – at least until 1787, when, on account of the new design of the prison, another aspect of criminal justice in Oxford was changed forever. Gone were the days of a temporary erection of a gibbet at Green Ditch, or use of the gallows within the castle grounds, and with them went the resultant violent disputes. With the gallows placed some 30 feet above the ground, on top of the main gateway leading to New Road (see FIGURE 16), such chaotic scenes became a thing of the past, and the doctors of anatomy could sharpen their knives with much greater confidence.

The first men to experience this "reformed mode" of execution were Thomas White, for stealing plate from Blenheim Palace, and Charles Walter Wyatt, for embezzlement. The event, on Monday 6 August 1787, inspired *Jackson's* to devote an unusually generous number of column inches to describing the new procedure.

At 4am, both men were summoned to the chapel, and there informed that the execution would be the same day, but that they could choose the hour themselves, between 8am and 12 noon. At 7am, the castle chaplain attended them, and at 9am "prisoners of every description" attended divine service. A strict fast was observed, and no work was permitted at the gaol for the whole day. At 11am, White and Wyatt's fetters were removed and the sacrament administered, after which the debtors returned to their apartments, while the other prisoners remained in the felons' yard (this being the other main innovation: that other convicts should be obliged to witness, and it was hoped, heed, the occasion). At 12 noon, the two men were taken from the chapel to the gallows with due respect for ceremony. The procession consisted of six of the sheriff's men "with javelins, two and two, the executioner, bareheaded, the two malefactors, in white caps and pinioned, between the turnkeys, armed, Redditch [Thomas], a condemned criminal, but reprieved, guarded by two constables, the rest of the felons, two and two, also guarded". To add to the sense of occasion, the bell of St Thomas' Church "tolled upwards of an hour and a half before and during the execution".

"THE PRISON IS A PALACE TODAY":
THOMAS DAVIS

The execution of White and Wyatt was the first to be held during Daniel Harris' tenure as governor. The last, on Monday 25 March 1805, was also a notable one, both on account of the detail which has survived of the procedure on the day, and the fact that the man in question was, for the first verifiable time, permitted to be interred immediately within the castle grounds. He was 43-year-old Thomas Davis. Davis was a religious dissenter, and it is the account of "the respectable minister of that society in this city", James Hinton, from which much of this intimate detail comes.* Hinton visited him most days, and recorded the results in a long printed letter entitled *A Narrative of the Behaviour and Death of Thomas Davis*. Davis had had scant religious instruction in his life, and was convinced that this was the cause of his downfall. Hinton concurred, but assured him that with true repentance it was not too late for spiritual salvation. Davis' final weeks were therefore more cheerful than for most who awaited death within the castle's condemned cell. Hinton quotes him as saying at one point: "I bless God night and day that I ever entered the walls of this prison. The little hope I feel that I shall obtain mercy gives a happiness to

* Davis had written to Hinton within a few days of his arrest for "having uttered a counterfeited note, purporting to be a one pound note ... with intent to defraud Elizabeth Cecil of Chipping Norton". Prison chaplains, or "ordinaries" as they were also called, were often the source or authors of the broadsheets published after executions, this being seen as reasonable recompense for the spiritual succour provided.

which none of the pleasure of sin can ever be compared. I never knew anything like happiness till now."

His morale was sustained to the last. On the day before the execution, Hinton joined him and two relatives to pray, sitting on the coffin in his cell as there was no other seat. Afterwards Davis said: "The prison is a palace today; this is surely somewhat like to Heaven. Do not let us weep any more. O! Blessed be God, for giving such a Sabbath as this for my last." Hinton stayed with Davis throughout the night. At 5am, workmen began to erect the platform. Hinton felt that "every stroke of the hammer reached my heart, but poor Davis heard the noise close to his cell without dismay". At 6.30am, both men walked from his cell to the chapel "which is at a short distance, and on the flat roof of which the platform as usual was erected". Soon after

> the executioner entered. He was attended by the proper officers, and he held out in his hand the *instrument of death*. A more terrific appearance I think no human form could assume. His keen eye rolled over the apartment in search of his victim. Davis calmly shook hands with him and said, "I am ready, do your duty."

Still in irons, Davis then ascended the long staircase to the scaffold unassisted. Hinton read out Davis' short admission of guilt and genuine penitence, then retired. A broadsheet summarised the scene in front of an "immense" number of spectators, "the generality of which shewed that pathetic feeling and compassion due to a relenting penitent" who was

> perfectly convinced that the hard earned shilling is far preferable to the guinea gained by fraudulence and deceit, and begs and most earnestly intreats all those who see or hear of his untimely death to be warned against that practice, and avoid avaricious desires, gambling, drinking, and all other baneful excesses, which lead on to speedy ruin and premature death, and entail a lasting disgrace on their memory, and an heart-breaking reflection to their innocent progeny.

The final act in this particularly poignant version of a familiar routine was described by *Jackson's* of 30 March 1805:

> The behaviour of the spectators was highly becoming the solemn occasion, and we understand that while the body was suspended, the prisoners who as usual witnessed the execution, were assembled in the chapel, and a very proper sermon preached to them, with great effect, by the regular chaplain. The body was immediately put in a coffin, which had been in the cell with him the whole of Sunday, and at his particular request, buried in a grave dug by his fellow prisoners, in the consecrated ground belonging to the chapel of St George within the walls of the castle.[*]

"The Protestant Joyner": Stephen Colledge

→>-<+-

The account of Thomas Davis' demise is unusual for the prominence given to the normally shadowy role of the executioner. These men, often prisoners themselves, are never named at the time, and rarely described. Only once in all the many executions which occurred at Oxford Castle is the hangman identified, and as the man in question was England's most famous executioner of all time, Jack Ketch, his appearance was of sufficient singularity to be worthy of terminating this narrative (see Appendix 3).

The execution that warranted the attention of Ketch was also unusual for another reason: it was one of very few known to have been conducted on a charge of treason. In the turbulent days of the latter seventeenth century, men found guilty of "treason" were as likely to have been framed as genuine, and more likely than not to have simply opted, however briefly, for the wrong Christian doctrine. Stephen Colledge, dubbed "the protestant joyner", may have fallen into that category. In London, where he was born in about 1635, his skill as a carpenter brought him into contact with

---

[*] *Jackson's* of 29 September 1798 mentions the consecration of "the new-built chapel of St George and burial ground within the walls of our Castle".

many people of rank, and encouraged his ambitions. But an ambitious man also attracts enemies, and when Colledge rode to Oxford in March 1681 (to coincide with the removal of Parliament from London to Oxford that month), ostentatiously advocating resistance to King Charles II, more than a few of these enemies took notice. As a result he found himself accused of seditious behaviour, and was committed to the Tower of London in June. His case was dismissed the following month – but not to the satisfaction of all. The government gathered additional evidence in relation to his activities in Oxford, and this time arranged for the trial to be held in Oxford, where it was felt that a jury might more readily follow the directions of the court lawyers. It did, finding Colledge guilty of the charge that "he prepared arms, armed himself, and incited and advised ... others to ... seize the person of the king at Oxford". His trial began at 8am on Wednesday 17 August, and lasted till 2am the following morning. Despite severe doubts about the veracity of the witnesses, and considerable contradictory evidence, the jury announced a guilty verdict after a further hour's deliberation. The actual sentence was withheld until 10am the following morning, when Colledge was summoned to hear the decision (as recorded in one of many contemporary commentaries on the case, *The Tryal of Stephen Colledge*):

> You shall be drawn on a hurdle to the place of execution, where you shall be hanged up by the neck, and be cut down alive, your privy members shall be cut off, and your bowels taken out and burnt before your face, your hand shall be cut off from your body, your body be divided into four quarters, which are to be at the king's dispose.

Colledge's response to hearing this cheering news was a simple "Amen".*

---

* The only concession was that Colledge was spared the common fate of posthumous public display. A broadsheet called *Dying Words of Stephen Colledge* (printed by his family, including Edith Colledge) concludes with: "About the 12 of the clock at noon he was executed and his head and quarters (through his Majesty's grace) delivered to his relations, and by them brought up to London, to be privately interred." George Napier (or Napper), whose family owned Holywell Manor, a known Catholic "safe house", was shown no such leniency after his own identical death in 1610. Anthony Wood said that his head and quarters were displayed upon the four gates of the city, and the one belonging to Christ Church, next to St Aldate's Church, "to the great terror of the Catholics that were then in and near Oxford".

The execution was delayed some days, in order, according to a barrister called Sir John Hawles (writing in 1689), to see "how the nation would digest the matter". He further observed that "tho' all people were quiet, yet there was great grumbling, and most honest men were afraid, and the constancy of Colledge at his execution was such that it made the most violent against him relent". On the fatal day, Wednesday 31 August, Colledge was executed against the gate of the castle. After embracing his son, and "kissing him several times with great passion", Colledge made a long speech, the contents of which can be summarised in one sentence, recorded in another pamphlet, *The Dying Words of Stephen Colledge* (printed by his own relations*) as: "I am reported to be a papist, I declare I was bred a protestant, such have I lived, and such I die."

And the man who made sure he died was Jack Ketch. A pamphlet entitled *The Speech and Carriage of Stephen Colledge at Oxford, before the Castle Wednesday August 31 1681*, identifies Ketch as the executioner, a fact confirmed by Anthony Wood. Although Ketch had a chequered career, being more famous for his bungled executions than for his successful ones, the fact that he travelled especially from his normal place of employment in London to attend to Colledge suggests that the government wanted to make a point. Or that no-one could be found in Oxford who was prepared to undertake an act about which many obviously had severe doubts. Whatever, the pamphlet's concluding words are: "The executioner, Ketch, desired his pardon, and he said, I do forgive you. The Lord have mercy on my soul."

The last public execution in Oxford occurred nearly two centuries later, on 23 March 1863, the same year that it was abolished as a public spectacle throughout the land. Noah Austin, a farmer's son from Upper Heyford, was hanged that day for murder, the only crime for which anyone was so punished in Oxford from 1836 onwards.

---

* According to Wood, he was the nephew of Edward Golledge (sic) of St Peter-le-Bailey, and his children were called Stephen and Edith.

"Doing time" to leisure time

-+->-<+-

This has been a sometimes uncomfortable history to write. From a distance of centuries, it is possible to overlook the fact that the people described were sentient, breathing human beings, rather than characters in a series of historical adventure stories. Human nature means that there will always be those who break the law, sometimes for reasons that are readily understood. Whatever the true natures of the criminals described in this book, one thing is clear, that the public spectacle of that final leap "into the unfathomable gulph of eternity" should be something forever confined to the annals of history. The Oxford Castle buildings now look forward to welcoming thousands of visitors a year. It remains to be seen if the experience is more like the "continual affrights and terrors" undergone by Anne Green in 1650 or "somewhat like to Heaven" as Thomas Davis found it in 1805. Whatever, it is to be hoped that visitors will take just a moment to consider the centuries of human suffering as well as ingenuity imbued in every stone of the historic buildings, and think themselves lucky. Unlike so many in the past, all that *we* have to do to leave the premises is to pay to the hotel or restaurant the modern-day equivalent of the gaoler's fees!

PUBLIC EXECUTIONS
IN OXFORD

In 1909 and 1926, a pamphlet called *The Hangman's Record* listed hundreds of English executions, under the claim of presenting "fuller details and more sensational items than has ever before been issued to the public". While lacking in sensation, the following pages do represent "fuller details" of Oxford executions than any other yet published. The principal sources are Anthony Wood's *City of Oxford* and *Life and Times* for executions held between 1587 and 1710; broadsheets and booklets held at the Bodleian Library between 1715 and 1752; and *Jackson's Oxford Journal* from 1753 onwards. All were hangings except Joanna (or Hannah) Mead in 1723. Place names are in Oxfordshire except where stated. All executions were held above the new main entrance to Oxford Castle in New Road from 1787 onwards.

(a) = anatomised

(x) = could be fictional

(∗) = died a prisoner, but not necessarily executed

c = executed at the Castle

GD = executed at Green Ditch

Date	Name	Age	Residence	Crime	Site	Notes
25 Oct 1587	**Harcourt Taverner**		Woodeaton	Highway robbery	c	Date buried St Martin's
1587	**? Woods**		Cumnor		c	Buried St Martin's
1604/05	**Richard Makepeace**		Witney		c	Buried St Thomas'
17 July 1607	**Leonard de Banke**		Minster Lovell		c	Date buried St Martin's
3 Oct 1609	**Robert de Banke** (*)		Minster Lovell		c	Date buried St Thomas'
9 Nov 1610	**George Napier (Napper)**		Oxford (Corpus Christi)	Treason	c	Hanged, drawn, and quartered
17 July 1612	**Thomas de Banke**		Minster Lovell		c	Date buried St Thomas'
12 Mar 1617/18	**Richard Busby**		Over Norton			Buried St Thomas'
?? Jan 1643/44	**Francis Cole**			"executed for a spie"		Buried St Clement's
14 Dec 1650	**Anne Green**	22	Steeple Barton	Infanticide	c	Date buried St Thomas'
22 Oct 1652	**Carpenter Carwardyn (Carrodin)**			Murder	c	Date buried St Thomas'
25 July 1654	**? Hussey**			Highway robbery	c	Date buried St Peter-le-Bailey
25 July 1654	**? Peck**			Highway robbery	c	Date buried St Peter-le-Bailey
4 May 1658	**Elizabeth ?**		Oxford	Infanticide	GD	
15 Mar 1670	**Ann Baxter**				c	Date buried St Thomas'
17 Mar 1675	**William Brewer**		Witney		c	
1 Mar 1676	**Richard Harber**		Worcestershire		c	
4 May 1680	**Alice Carpenter**		Botley	Infanticide	GD	
31 Aug 1681	**Stephen Colledge**		London	Treason	c	Born Watford, buried London
7 April 1688	**John Cornet(t)**	30		Murder	c	French
20 Mar 1697	**William Aldridge**					Date buried St Thomas'
20 Mar 1697	**John Collett**					Date buried St Thomas'
20 Mar 1697	**Thomas Minshon**					Date buried St Thomas'
30 Mar 1698	**John Sones**					Date buried St Thomas'
3 April 1710	**Thomas Sprignell** (*)					Date buried St Thomas'

Date	Name	Age	Residence	Crime	Site	Notes
19 Aug 1715	Richard Groom		Oxford	Receiving	c	Buried Witney?
19 Aug 1715	?? (female)		Garsington?	Theft	c	Source: Hearne
1716	Sarah (?) Sparrow[(x)]		Oxford	Infanticide		
17 May 1723	Hannah or Joanna Mead	24	Combe	Murder of husband	GD	Burned. Source: Hearne
22 Mar 1725	John Protheroe	33	Barton	Murder of wife	c	Born Evesham, 1692. Source: Hearne
1735/36	Jonathan Bradford [(x)]		Golden Ball Inn	Murder		Inn on Oxford to Wallingford road
1 Sept 1749	Paul Wells, gent.	35	Cuddesdon	Forgery		Buried Cuddesdon
6 April 1752	Mary Blandy	33	Henley	Patricide	c	Buried Henley
1753?	William Grindy			Transportation returnee		Buried St Thomas'?
4 Feb 1754	Margaret Dunn			Theft	GD	
22 Mar 1754	Acton Brice			Highway robbery	GD	
22 Mar 1754	Richard Bayliss			Highway robbery	GD	
26 April 1754	James Till [(a)]	17		Theft	GD	
21 Mar 1755	Richard Mansfield	20		Highway robbery		
21 Mar 1755	Richard Dancer	19		Highway robbery		
28 April 1755	Robert Randall			Sheep-stealing	c	
23 April 1757	John Franklin [(a)]		Oxford	Murder of wife	GD	
20 Mar 1758	William Hardiman [(a)]			Highway robbery		
23 Mar 1761	Isaac Darkin (Dumas)	20	London	Highway robbery	c	Buried St Thomas'?
22 Mar 1762	Shadrack Smith [(a)]	59	Charlbury	Theft	c	Born Norwood, Essex
24 July 1762	James Costard [(a)]		Benson	Matricide		
24 July 1762	Susan Harris [(a)]		Sydenham	Infanticide		
22 April 1765	Parker Hall		Oxford	Theft	c	
10 Mar 1766	Mary Lampry		Kingham	Infanticide (of grandchild)		
28 July 1766	John Milward (Brown)		Northants.	Highway robbery		

Date	Name	Age	Residence	Crime	Site	Notes
28 July 1766	John Williams			Highway robbery		Born Beckley, Northants. Brother of James (below)
23 Mar 1772	Richard Gardner	30	Witney?	Theft		
13 Mar 1775	George Strap [a]		Bicester	Murder		Born Camsey, Worcs.
14 Aug 1775	James Corbett			Theft		
9 Mar 1777	Robert Hitchcock [a]	40	Combe	Patricide		
22 Mar 1779	William Hyde	32	Stanton St John	Theft		Buried Stanton St John
30 Aug 1780	Richard Wells	33	Bampton	Sheep- & horse-theft		Buried Bampton
8 Mar 1784	Daniel Cato [a]		Hook Norton	Murder		
22 Mar 1784	Benjamin Webb (Crawford)	38	Salford, Bath	Theft		
22 Mar 1784	George Ward (Dagger)	28	Bitton, Glos.	Theft		
30 Mar 1784	Giles Freeman			Highway robbery		
27 Mar 1786	John Cox	31	Henley	Theft and sheep-stealing		Brother of Richard, buried Henley
27 Mar 1786	Richard Cox	21	Henley	Theft and sheep-stealing		Brother of John, buried Henley
27 Mar 1786	John Grace	24		Sheep-stealing		
27 Mar 1786	Miles Ward	21	London	Theft		
6 Aug 1787	Thomas White		Blenheim Palace	Theft		Buried St Thomas'
6 Aug 1787	Charles Walter Wyatt	19	Witney	Embezzlement		
24 Mar 1788	Charles Smith	28		Horse-theft		
22 Mar 1790	Thomas Smith (Davis)		London	Horse-theft		
19 July 1790	John C [a]	31/35	Abingdon	Murder		
19 July 1790	Charles Evans Shury [a]	42	Abingdon	Murder		
2 Aug 1790	James Williams	30/34		Horse-theft		Born Beckley, brother of John (above)
7 Mar 1791	Giles Freeman Covington [a]	23	Abingdon	Murder		Skeleton is at Oxford Museum
21 Mar 1791	John Daves (Kelly)	27		Highway robbery		Born Carmarthenshire
26 Mar 1792	Joseph Tapp	29		Highway robbery		

Date	Name	Age	Residence	Crime	Site	Notes
29 July 1793	Robert Jenkinson			Horse-theft		
21 Aug 1796	John Marshall	32		Horse-theft		Born Durham
21 Aug 1796	Thomas Andrews	37/39		Horse-theft		Born Daylesford, near Chipping Norton
21 Aug 1796	William Use	24		House-breaking		Born Manchester
26 Mar 1798	James Carpenter	23/24		House-breaking		
28 July 1800	Edward Thorn	59	Henley	Murder		Born Steventon
23 Mar 1801	Jesse Wiggins	45		Sheep-stealing		
25 Mar 1805	Thomas Davis	43		Counterfeiting		Born Droitwich
10 July 1815	James Bannister			Murder of wife		Source: Jackson's of 6/4/1878
26 Mar 1817	William Archer			Arson		"
2 Aug 1818	John Bradley			Highway robbery		"
2 Aug 1818	Richard Wiggins			Sheep-stealing		"
5 Aug 1822	John Matthews			Highway robbery		"
1 Aug 1824	William James			Murder		"
1 Aug 1824	Henry Pittaway			Murder		"
20 Mar 1826	William Clack	21		Horse-theft		"
26 Mar 1827	Richard Webbe			Horse-theft		"
23 Mar 1828	Thomas Shaler			Highway robbery		"
19 Mar 1832	John Gibbs			Arson		"
19 Mar 1832	George Lay (Keats)			Attempted murder		"
5 Mar 1836	Thomas Clay			Murder		"
23 Mar 1840	Charles Morley			Murder		"
22 Mar 1852	William Kalabergo			Murder		"
23 Mar 1863	Noah Austin			Murder		"

APPENDIX 2

GREEN DITCH

The execution site at Green Ditch was at the one mile stone on the Banbury Road. The ditch itself was about four feet wide and three deep (running along that part of today's St Margaret's Road which runs between the Woodstock and Banbury Roads), and marked the northern extent of the Oxford city franchise. It appears to have been used as a place of execution from very early times. The first implied reference was in 1285, according to Margaret Gelling's *Place Names of Oxfordshire*, and in 1375 Green Ditch was distinguished as the location of the town gallows when they were overturned by members of the University (which had its own place of execution at Holywell). Some rebels against Henry IV were executed there in 1400.

It would seem, therefore, that the site had been used as the location for executions of Oxford townsmen long before Dr Robert Plot defined the location (in *The Natural History of Oxfordshire*, 1705) as "the place appointed for the execution of the city malefactors" (as opposed to those coming from elsewhere in the county). Certainly, the cost of erecting a gallows tree there was a city council responsibility, appearing in the chamberlain's accounts in 1616, 1629/30, 1634/35, and 1657/58. The latter cost was for £1 12s 6d, "for making a pair of gallows and setting of them up at Green Ditch and for cutting down a tree and bring it home". If one reads this to mean that one set of gallows was taken back to Oxford, the set left standing must have been those used for the failed hanging on 4 May 1658 of Elizabeth, Mrs Cope's maid, described in Chapter Five.

Others known to have been executed at Green Ditch are Alice Carpenter of Botley on 4 May 1680, for killing her bastard child, an unnamed soldier whose hanging on Friday 24 May 1717 was noted by

Thomas Hearne, and three people whose deaths featured in *Jackson's Oxford Journal*.

The first of these was Margaret Dunn. *Jackson's* report of her execution on Monday 4 February 1754 stated that the gallows had been "erected for that purpose", indicating that the structure was not permanent by this time – and possibly never was. Dunn had been arrested for a theft committed three years earlier, but had escaped from prison, and was taken again the month before her execution. Behaving "with amazing intrepidity", she "spoke near half an hour at the place of execution, and confessed herself to have been involved in all kinds of wickedness except murder, to which detestable crime she professed the utmost abhorrence". Of all the people executed at Oxford in the eighteenth century, she is the only one whose religious belief is specified, namely Roman Catholicism.

The youngest person known to have been executed in Oxford was 17-year-old James Till, and it was at Green Ditch, on Friday 26 April 1754, that he met his end. The following week, *Jackson's* printed a letter from an unnamed University source, though it would be no surprise to learn that it was written by or on behalf of an anatomist. The writer stated that Till's body had been "regularly delivered to the gentlemen of the University for the purpose of anatomical lectures" without incident. This the writer attributed to the presence of "several stout, resolute persons … with orders to lay hold of, and secure in the castle, any person or persons who should make the least attempt towards carrying off the body". This measure was deemed necessary on account of the rioters who had carried away the bodies of the two persons executed (seemingly also at Green Ditch) about a month previously (i.e. two highwaymen called Acton Brice and Richard Bayliss). The writer also thought that dissection should be

extended to *all* malefactors in general, since, if the consigning of the bodies of murderers to this use may be expected to have a good influence towards preventing murders, no reason can be assigned why the like good effects may not be expected from the like penalty annexed to other capital offences.

By a law of 1751, the bodies of murderers were automatically made available for dissection. But only murderers. As Till himself had been found guilty only of stealing money from his master, and Brice and Bayliss of highway robbery (capital offences though these were), it would seem that the anatomists had in any case already taken the law into their own hands in this respect. Murderers were rare in Oxfordshire, leaving the students of anatomy at Oxford desperate for specimens. One can therefore understand why violence marked the end of many executions at this time (epitomised by the cases of Robert Randall in 1755 and Isaac Darkin in 1761). The tug-of-war between relatives with moral and legal right on their side and agents of the anatomists with the weight of authority on theirs is as unsavoury an aspect of these executions as any.

There was no such dispute at the last execution definitely held at Green Ditch, on Saturday 23 April 1757, because John Franklin was a self-confessed murderer. The victim had been his own pregnant wife, and his body was claimed by the anatomists without resistance. Franklin was a member of "a gang who lurk about and infest the country, cloaking their villainies under pretence of getting a livelihood by horsetaking" (where men would endeavour to retrieve stolen horses in order to claim a reward, as with "thief-takers". It was a less than respected profession, often used as a cover for actual horse theft). With misguided optimism, Franklin was known to have entertained bets of two and three to one that he would be acquitted. And there must indeed have been some possibility of him winning that bet, since the trial lasted five hours. Unusually, the time of Franklin's execution was late in the day, *Jackson's* observing that he was "put in the cart about four o'clock in the afternoon wherein he stood upright and read very loud and distinct all the way to Green Ditch". At the gallows he "continued reading and praying aloud without the least hesitation for an hour with amazing spirits". Then "the cart drew away ..."

John Franklin is the last person known to have been executed at Green Ditch, but it appears that the practice continued for at least a further 20 years, as Sir John Peshall, writing in 1773 (in *The Antient and Present State of the City of Oxford*), referred to "*Greenditch, or Woditch*, where the city gallows stood, but now are occasionally placed". From 1787 onwards, Green Ditch was certainly no longer used for this purpose, in view of the much preferred location above the gateway to the newly rebuilt prison. Its former purpose was commemorated into the next century, however, an 1827 map of St Giles' parish at the Bodleian Library (MS C17:70 Oxford 53) referring to "Gallows Baulk Road". More recently, when the flats known today as Murray Court (84–88 Banbury Road) were first occupied in 1997, the name then selected was "Grenediche House".

JACK KETCH AND
SOME OXFORD HANGMEN

Jack Ketch (otherwise known as John Catch) achieved fame during his lifetime as a long-standing London executioner of noted brutality, and immortality after his death as the character of the hangman in the Punch and Judy puppet shows. Ketch is thought to have taken office in 1663, although the first written reference to him appeared only in 1670, when a prisoner in the Tower of London, John Ellwood, provided a first-hand description (reproduced in Geoffrey Abbott's 1991 *Lords of the Scaffold*) of what he called "Jack Ketch's Kitchen". This was a small closet or alcove near Ellwood's cell, where the quartered bodies of three recently executed men were being stored while their relatives negotiated for their return. These were duly relinquished – but without the heads, which were destined for public display. In order to preserve them, Ketch boiling the heads overnight in a solution of bay salt and cumin seed, an experience which Ellwood understandably found "both frightful and loathsome". His fellow prisoners seemed to have no such sensitivities: before placing the heads in his pots, Ketch made sport with them, to the mutual merriment of all.

In 1678 a broadsheet was published with the title *The Plotters Ballad, being Jack Ketch's incomparable Receipt* [i.e. recipe] *for the Cure of Traytorous Recusants*. It is illustrated with a woodcut in which a condemned Catholic called Edward Coleman says, "I am sick of a traytorous disease." Ketch is shown, with a hatchet in one hand and a rope in the other, saying, "Here is your cure, sir."

Ketch is an example of a prisoner-turned-executioner, having been imprisoned in the notorious debtors' prison of Marshalsea (in Southwark), the other side of the river from his home in Spreadeagle Alley, near Bow Street. Two years after his visit to Oxford for the execution of Stephen Colledge, his services were required to attend to Lord William Russell, arraigned for high treason in connection with a supposed Catholic plot to assassinate Charles II. The beheading on 21 July 1683 was badly bungled, and Ketch was obliged to issue a public apology. His dispatch on 15 July 1685 of the Duke of Monmouth (Charles II's illegitimate son) after his failed rebellion was even more inexpert, and sealed Ketch's reputation for ineptitude; his frequent contributions to the reprisals against Monmouth's followers later that year (characterised by Judge Jeffreys and the "Bloody Assizes") sealed his reputation for brutality.

Ketch was briefly replaced as executioner in January 1686 for causing affront to the Sheriff of London, but was reinstated in May, his replacement, Pascha Rose, having himself been executed earlier that month. Ketch died before the end of the same year, and was buried at St James', Clerkenwell on 29 November 1686. His wife had remained loyal in the face of almost universal execration, if the dramatist John Dryden is any guide. He said in 1693 that: "A man may be capable, as Jack Ketch's wife said of his servant, of a plain piece of work, a bare hanging, but to make a malefactor die sweetly was only belonging to her husband." This quote comes from *The Punch and Judy Show* by Robert Leach (1985), from which the following paragraph also derives.

After his death, Ketch's notoriety was such that his name very quickly became a generic term. He more than any other hangman was identified with the brutal oppression of the state, and his absorption into Punch and Judy comes as a result of the contemporaneous appearance of the show in England. Introduced from Italy in the latter seventeenth century, the anglicised name of Punch had been adopted by the 1680s, when Ketch was at the height of his fame. Punch is an unashamedly violent character, yet he is also the hero of the piece. His situation represented the constraint of individual freedom by family, religion, and state. Punch's victory over Ketch constituted his resistance to the latter, when, facing the gallows for (in most versions) killing Judy, he pretends not to know how to fix the noose. The gullible Ketch eventually demonstrates the technique himself, at which point Punch kicks away the ladder. This scene, according to Bernard Blackmantle in *The English Spy* (1826), is "the *ne plus ultra* of his comicalities … Mr John Ketch hangs suspended in the air – Punch shouts a glorious triumph – all the world backs him in his conquest." It is a scene which captures the reality of many executions, where the criminal, a free man rebelling against the unfair strictures of society, was the hero while the hangman, the agent of state oppression, was the villain.

HANGMEN OF OXFORD

Whether Ketch's name would have lived on had it not been popularised by this enduring puppet show is a moot point. Certainly *Jackson's Oxford Journal* considered that its readers would be familiar with the allusion a whole century after his death. When Robert Jenkinson was executed on Monday 29 July 1793 for horse-theft, the newspaper observed succinctly: "He had been fervent in prayer previous to his being brought out, but was totally silent at the place of execution, and the moment Jack Ketch had fixed the halter the drop took place."

The true names of only two Oxford executioners are known. *Jackson's* reported on 26 April 1760 that the hangman James Crozier had enlisted in the army. With sometimes baffling use of italics, the newspaper took the opportunity to inject some levity into sentiments which reflected the sad inevitability of continuing lawlessness. Crozier,

> who in the *execution* of that office, has *put to death* many magnanimous *heroes*, inlisted himself into one of the new in-*dependent* companies. Probably at the end of the war, when his services *abroad* shall become unnecessary, he may at *home* find sufficient employment in his old profession.

The other named Oxford hangman was William Blackhall. When he was committed to the castle charged with stealing "the carcass of a dead fat hog" in Henley in March 1787, *Jackson's* noted that he had "on a former occasion officiated as hangman" (*Jackson's* 3 March 1787).

It is supposed that many executioners were themselves prisoners. Certainly this was true in the cases of Anne Green in 1650 and Isaac Darkin in 1761. It appears that Blackhall too may have fallen into this category. Crozier was evidently a "professional", though – or at least someone who undertook the role on a regular basis. The man who executed Richard Gardner (for numerous robberies and burglaries in Witney) on Monday 23 March 1772 seems to have been a bit of both: brought in especially for the purpose, yet of evident criminal tendencies, as this from *Jackson's* of 28 March 1772 shows:

> The fellow who officiated as hangman, being lodged the preceding night in one of the rooms of the dwelling house belonging to the keeper, was so little affected by Gardner's approaching catastrophe that he stole a pair of plated buckles and two handkerchiefs, but finding himself suspected, he threw down the handkerchiefs and pretended innocence.

This is as clear an example as any of the impotence of capital punishment. If the authorities intended the sight of a felon expiring in torments of terror and agony to be a frightful warning to those watching, they were mistaken: the crowds positively enjoyed the experience. And if the authorities expected that imposing the death penalty for crimes as trivial as stealing a handkerchief would deter all thieves, they were also wrong. If the lesson was not heeded by the hangman, that intimate witness of those last horrifying moments of ebbing life, then who on earth would?

Sources and further reading

BOARDMAN, CARL — *Oxfordshire Sinners and Villains*, Alan Sutton, 1994

Foul Deeds and Suspicious Deaths Around Oxfordshire, Wharncliffe Books, 2004

COLDHAM, PETER WILSON — *The Complete Book of Emigrants in Bondage 1614–1775*, Genealogical Publishing Co., Baltimore, 1988

COX, G.V. — *Recollections of Oxford* (2nd edition), Macmillan, 1870

CROSSLEY, ALAN (ed.) — *Victoria History of the County of Oxford* (volume iv), Oxford University Press, 1979

DAVENPORT, J.M. — *Notes As To Oxford Castle*, Oxford County Hall, 1877

GOVE, PHILIP BABCOCK — *An Oxford Convict in Maryland* from The Maryland Historical Review (June 1942)

GREEN, JOHN RICHARD — *Oxford Studies*, Macmillan, 1901

HIBBERT, C. & E. (eds.) — *Encyclopaedia of Oxford*, Macmillan, 1988

HOWARD, JOHN — *The State of the Prisons In England and Wales etc.*, William Eyres, Warrington, 1777, 1780, & 1782 (editions one to three)

The State of the Prisons In England and Wales etc., Johnson, Dilly, & Cadell, London, 1792 (4th edition)

Appendix to The State of the Prisons In England and Wales etc., William Eyres, Warrington, 1784

An Account of the Principal Lazarettos of Europe etc., William Eyres, Warrington, 1789

KING, EDWARD   *Vestiges of Oxford Castle*, George Nicol, London, 1796

NICHOLS, JOHN (ed.)   *Literary Anecdotes of the Eighteenth Century Vol III*,
                           John Nichols, 1812

PLOT, DR ROBERT   *The Natural History of Oxfordshire ...*" (2nd edition),
                           Charles Brome & John Nicholson, London, 1705

SQUIRES, THOMAS   *In West Oxford: Historical Notes and Pictures Concerning the
                           Parish of St Thomas the Martyr*, Mobray, 1928

THOMPSON, J. M.   *The Robbery from the Ashmolean Museum*, 1776 (1931) and
                           Le Maitre, alias Marat (1934) in *English Historical Review*

Index of main names and places*

➤➤◄◄

Places in **bold** appear in map on pages viii and ix